RESIDENT EVIL VILLAGE

COMPLETE GUIDE

DEANNA TREFZ

Copyright © 2021 Deanna Trefz

All rights reserved.

ISBN: 9798510379211

Contents

Prologue - The Winters House 1

The Village (Arrival) 2

Castle Dimitrescu 11

The Village (Second Visit) 30

House Beneviento 37

The Village (Third Visit) 44

The Reservoir 48

The Village (Fourth Visit) 57

The Stronghold 63

Heisenberg's Factory 67

Finale 82

How to Hide From Lady Dimitrescu 87

How to Open Castle Dimitrescu's Gate 90

How to Get the Courtyard Key 91

How to Open Iron Insignia Doors 92

How to Get The Prison Treasure 92

How to Get The Maestro's Collection 93

How to Get The Waterwheel Weapon 94

How to Get Luiza's Heirloom 94

How to Get Beneviento's Treasure 95

How to Get Moreau's Hidden Weapon 96

How to Get to the Riverbank Treasure House 97

How to Get Cannibal's Plunder 99

How to Get The Treasure Under the Stronghold 100

How to Get the Relief of a Horse 101

How to Get the Cog Mold 101

How to Complete the Necklace With Two Holes 102

How to Get the Well Wheel 103

How to Pick Locks 104

How to Unlock Infinite Ammo 105

Tips and Tricks 106

Resident Evil Village crystal fragments, treasure locations, and how to get more money fast 109

Resident Evil Village - how to survive the attack at the start 113

Resident Evil Village statue puzzle solution 115

Resident Evil Village piano puzzle solution - how to press the right keys 115

How to solve the Resident Evil Village bell puzzle and ring all five bells 116

8 Resident Evil Village Tips & Tricks That Will Help You Survive the Horror 118

14 tips for surviving Resident Evil Village 121

15 Tips and Tricks to Keep in Mind 124

10 Things Only Pro Players Know You Can Do In Resident Evil Village 128

10 Things That Make No Sense In Resident Evil Village 131

10 Hidden Areas In Resident Evil Village Everyone Completely Missed 134

10 Things We Wish We Knew Before Starting Resident Evil Village 137

Prologue - The Winters House

After the opening story-book cutscene, you'll find yourself in the new family home of Ethan and Mia Winters, as well as their new baby girl, Rosemary. Having survived the events at the Baker Estate, the couple has been placed into a sort of witness protection program, and living a new peaceful life somewhere in Eastern Europe - though Mia seems loathe to speak of their traumatic incident.

Take Rose to Bed

With your baby in hand, you can feel free to explore your home, and spy several interactive objects.

There's a remote by the nearby TV to turn on some cartoons, some baby books, framed photos, and music CDs in the dining room.

Further up you can bug Mia in the kitchen, or check the fridge for Fridge Memo File, as well as some extra baby food in the pantry. Out in the front hallway, you can spot a framed photo of Rose, as well as her stroller before you head upstairs.

At the top of the stairs, you can inspect a music box on the left, and a bathroom on the right full of Mia's medication. Head down the nearby hall and you'll enter the main bedroom where you can drop off Rose to sleep.

Before leaving, be sure to look around for some of Rose's clothes, and an adjoining den with a computer that holds Ethan's Diary File, and next to it in a drawer you can find the Medical Checkup Report File. On the other side there's a bookshelf with a little reference to a famous gunsmith, and on the right is a photo book full of Ethan and Mia's life together.

Before heading back downstairs, you can also check out the far room above the stairs going back down to explore an unused bedroom with a bookshelf, and a newspaper on a table with the Old News Clipping File.

Achievement/Trophy Note - Remember there are some areas with collectibles that you cannot return to, so be sure to grab the aforementioned Files before concluding this prologue!

When you're ready to conclude this prologue, head back to Mia to enjoy dinner - before a familiar guest rudely comes calling, and events will quickly unfold leaving your family shattered, and your fate unknown.

The Village (Arrival)

After being abducted by Chris Redfield and his mysterious team, you'll awaken in the snow next to a dead body and the remains of the vehicle you were being hauled off in. Answering the dead man's phone provides little clues as to what's going on - and your only real course of action is to find shelter.

Reach the Village

Note that at this point, you can finally access your map and journal, and you can keep track of Ethan's thoughts in his small diary entries, as well as reviewing the Files you have found so far.

File.

Follow the indented trail someone has left leading away from the crash into the dark woods. You won't be able to make much out as you advance, so try not to let the sounds of something lurking close by get to you.

Once you reach a dead end, crouch down to scramble under some barbed wire, and then onward through an ominous group of hanged birds until you can drop down to an area below. You may even notice something moving ahead of you - don't worry about it for now, just keep moving forward until you cross a small footbridge and the image of a foreboding home comes into view.

The blood on the floor and doorway isn't the most welcoming sign, but there's little else to do but enter the creepy house. Note that you can open a drawer on the right as you advance - it may be empty, but it's worth checking every interactive object as you move forward to find useful items.

Stop the leaky sink or pass by it as you move into the next room to find a similarly empty cupboard, and then turn and follow the blood trail into the hall leading down to a basement.

As you move through the confines of the lower rooms, look for a face down framed picture of an ominous figure you can find on a table - its a face you'll be seeing more of later on.

Speaking of ominous things, a pile of wooden planks will fall down as you proceed, and you can turn left to see they were obscuring a very disturbing sketch of a being with four wings on the wall.

Open the spooky looking cabinet at the end of the room to find - nothing. However it won't be long before a commotion occurs up above you, prompting you to return the way you came.

A dresser will have been knocked in front of the door back to the main room, so crouch down to crawl under to find the place in shambles - and a giant hole in the side of the house. Exit through the new hole to find the sky a bit lighter outside, and follow the clear path away from the home and lean into the fence to jump over it.

As you finally make it to a clearing, you'll see a very spooky looking castle perched above a small and empty looking village, as bells ring out across the valley - almost as if heralding your arrival to the village.

West Old Town

From your vantage point, look around to start dropping down ledges to enter the outskirts of the village proper. As you enter the west side of the town, you'll come upon a gruesome sight of a slain horse near a large home. From here you can cut across the road to the left, or explore the home to your right.

The main doorway leads to a room with a locked drawer, and a destroyed area with another creepy mural on the floor. The other door leads to a narrow kennel leading to a small area with a well and outhouse - but you can't interact with the well just yet. There's also a small barn-like building with chains along the wall - and a yellow birdcage hanging from the ceiling, remember that.

Since you can't head to the right through the padlocked gate, go left down the street instead to come upon a dilapidated and blood-soaked house. There's another creepy mural here, as well as an outhouse around the corner.

Continue along the main road leading right past the broken house to find a damaged tractor and a bunch of dangling animal heads - very welcoming. Note the signposts pointing out that the path to the Graveyard and Ceremony Site is blocked, and turn left to find another padlocked home, and a large house with an open doorway. There's a curious gate to the side, but as you can expect in a Resident Evil game, many doors can only be opened by specific means.

Entering the large foreboding house, you should notice a yellow-splashed crate on the right - and further up is the tool to break it open, a Knife. You can now destroy the crate to get a First Aid Med.

Note: you no longer need to specifically equip the knife to break crates, you need only interact with them. Most all crates and breakable objects you find from then on will usually contain either money, crafting resources, or ammo, so always look for the yellow splashes on objects

Unfortunately, a commotion from above means you won't be able to go back out the way you came, so instead move into the kitchen. As you move to inspect the pot of soup, you may notice a solitary can rolling out from the pantry.

Inspect the curtain to meet a lone survivor, one who will give you another weapon, a LEMI Handgun, in a futile attempt to help save his doomed life.

As unknown assailants snatch up the villager, you'll be pulled into a similar scenario, coming to rest in a cellar full of corpses. Not great. Make your way along the bodies and move them aside to find a way out - only to finally spot one of the assailants - a Lycan. This altered human will take a bite out of you, and toss you outside for your first real combat session.

Lycans are cagey fighters - unlike zombies or even the molded, Lycans will close the distance quickly before stopping a few feet away to try to jump to the side or duck down as they advance upon you, and may even sometimes wield weapons. If they get too close, they'll try to lunge and take a bite out of you - in which case you'll need to press down the block button right before they hit to absorb most of the impact, and tap the block button again to shove them back. Doing so will stun them for a brief moment, allowing you to get off a quick headshot before they can begin moving again. Lycans aren't exactly fragile either, and you may have to expend several bullets to take one down.

After the first Lycan finally goes down, it's time to move on. If you've been injured greatly, look for a nearby shack from the house you were thrown out of and check the shelves for Chem Fluid and a Herb. Using both these items, you can go into your crafting menu and make First Aid Med if you need to.

In order to continue, look to the nearby gate to find it padlocked with a chain, but you'll need something to cut through. Return to the house where you found the lone survivor, and check the back of the pantry he was hiding in to find Bolt Cutters. Now you can return and open the gate into the next part of the Village.

East Old Town

Moving through the gate, you can cross a small river that's blocked on both sides - and enter a large barn-type building. Inside you'll hear the noise of radio static - but it will stop as soon as you approach, around the time something thumps upstairs. Be sure to pick up the Handgun Ammo by the window, then move to the stairs and make your way up to the top. There's more Handgun Ammo up here, as well as Chem Fluid on the floor - but as soon as you grab them, Lycans will appear outside.

Note the shelves near the front door - they can be used to provide a temporary barrier to stop Lycans from getting in, but in this sequence, you'll only need to worry about one that slips in through the wall above the stairs.

Be ready to unload a clip and backpedal, and block his attack to shove him back and try to get in a few headshots.

Once this single Lycan is defeated, the rest will retreat away from the doors and windows, and you'll get a temporary reprieve. Before leaving, walk back over to the radio, and you'll get a message that survivor's should head to a specific house on the other side of the Village by the fields.

Exit the house cautiously, and you'll find the barricades to the left have been torn down, and there's a bloody trail leading to the nearby house. You can spot Lycans watching you from the rooftops - but for the moment they'll just watch. Best to keep it that way and not fire on them just yet. Take the time to go around the back of the barn you were just in and open the back gate to create another path.

Approach the house the Lycans are on top of, and smash the nearby crate for loot. Now head up the short stairs and note the window into the house looks in on a weapon well worth getting.

However, as soon as you move into the home, the Lycans will drop down to charge you. Waste no time in barricading the door, and grabbing the M1897 Shotgun off the table. While the room is still barricaded, look for a Herb in the corner, and Gunpowder and Handgun Ammo near the door in a drawer, before moving to the next room. Here, you'll find more Handgun Ammo and Gunpowder, as well as stacks of flour you can strike to create a blinding cloud.

Since your enemies are not going to stop coming, it's better to get out into the open once more, so look for a hole to drop into, and dart down a narrow cellar to grab some Rusted Scrap and then leave. Now that the Lycans are after you, this next part is all about survival - which means you'll need to run and gun, but cautiously so.

Don't waste all your ammo right at once, and use the buildings, river, and back alleys to lead the Lycans on a chase to try and stay one step ahead of them. Remember to barricade doors, look for ladders, as well as a TNT barrel near the barred red gate to lure a group of

Lycans close before shooting it to deal massive damage at the cost of a single bullet.

You can also check the highest house above the stream to find another TNT barrel inside along with Shotgun Ammo, a Herb, and a barricade, as well as a breakable crate, and an escape ladder up to the roof.

Unfortunately, an even larger Lycan, Urias, will soon join the fray with a giant hammer - and this is one enemy you do not want to get near. Give it a wide berth, unless you're feeling gutsy, at which point you can try sprinting past the creature before it can lay the hammer down, and may sometimes damage its friends by mistake.

After enough time has passed, you'll either get hit by an arrow, or a Lycan will randomly grab you and toss you into the stream before they surround you. Luckily, it seems this is not your time to die, and the group will move off - as your attention turns to a mysterious old woman moving up past the large red gate.

Before following her, be sure to do one last sweep of the alleys and homes here to get any items you missed, like the crates by the homes'.

Village Square

- Find a Way to Open the Castle Gate

As you catch up with the old crone, she'll give you a cryptic warning while mentioning that your daughter is indeed in the clutches of the nefarious forces in the nearby castle. However, you're going to need to find a way to get there.

Start by checking the large home to the left of the Maiden of War statue, where you'll find another creepy mural on the floor of the room, and Chem Fluid and a Scribbled Note File. Check under the bed for some Lei, and there's also a locked drawer here - but we can't do anything about that for now.

Entering the Village Square, check the Maiden of War statue in the center. If you look close, you can spot a gleam on the shield - and shooting it with your handgun will cause a Crystal Fragment to drop - a very expensive treasure you can sell later. Be sure to also get the Gunpowder on a bloodstained bench, Rusted Scrap on a ruined tractor, and note the other sealed off areas here.

Goat of Warding - As you move up the path to the Graveyard, note the small shrine on the right with a wooden goat figurine that bobbles up and down making a distinct noise. These are a type of collectible you can destroy (no use worrying about Mother Miranda's wrath if they all want you dead anyway). Many of these goats are often found in places you might not be able to get to later, so always keep an eye (and an ear) out when exploring new areas. Be sure to also read the Goat of Warding Engraving File below the goat itself.

Be sure to inspect the Graveyard for a locked mausoleum with something inside, and check the far back to find a Herb by one of the gravestones. Further up you'll locate a large castle gate, but it's missing two circular crests - which means you now have a real objective.

Before checking out the church on the right, look for a small path following a sign for a Stronghold only to find a locked door with that eerie winged fetus mural. As you turn back, look up into the tree branches to spot a yellow birdcage, and shoot it down to collect another Rusted Scrap.

Goat of Warding - As you enter the yard with the church, be sure to look up onto the roof of the building, and checking the left side, you should spot another Goat of Warding perched on top that you can snipe.

Moving along into the large church area, you can head inside to find your first real Save Point, a Typewriter! While you're here, you can claim the first Maiden Crest at the front of a shrine, and you'll notice a large depiction of that framed photo you found earlier, along with 4 other photos which can only be the head honchos of this land. Get a good look at them - this won't be the last you see of them. You can also look along the photos on the wall above the shrine to see another Crystal Fragment you can shoot down and collect.

As for the other crest, look on a nearby chair to spot a map of the village, showing the other crest is nearby at the very same house you heard the radio told you to come to. You can reach it by looking for a path to the right of the church, where a large field separates you from the other house.

Before making the dangerous journey through the Fallow Plot, look for a nearby shack on the left and inspect the rooms to find Gunpowder, Rusted Scrap, Handgun Ammo in a drawer, and a Mine.

The Mine can be placed on the ground as a trap to lure enemies into - which you can test just outside if you like.

The field is alive with rustling, as three Lycans are darting through the tall grass. They won't come out in the open however - at least until you either get close enough, or manage to hit them from a distance with your pistol. If you do see them before entering the field, you may want to try luring one out at a time, and either gun them down as they leave the field, or lure them into a mine. You can also retreat into a smaller shack that holds some Rusted Scrap and Shotgun Ammo.

Move through the field when you're ready, and seek out a lone crate holding on a rock in a small clearing - which can give you room to look around at approaching threats, as well as another crate further back against the fence. You can also lure the Lycans towards the bags of flour, and strike them to blind your attackers for several moments, giving you plenty of free time to unload your handgun. Look up at the big tree in the field to spy a birdcage that can be shot down to get yourself 1,000 Lei.

Note - If you're low on ammo, you can always try to sprint past the lycans to the top of the road and enter the door on the right - they won't be able to follow!

Goat of Warding - if you stick to the far left side of the Fallow Plot, you can hop a small fence and move up a small path to a stone wall behind a shack. Though it's a dead end, look on the stone wall to spot another wooden goat you can shoot with your handgun.

When the enemies have been dealt with, or you choose to run past them, look for a small home to the right of the sealed gate at the top of the field, and enter to find more survivors hiding inside. They are also trying to get to Luiza's house if not for the locked gate. You'll need to help them find a way inside.

Start by hopping out the open window on the other side of the room, and break open the nearby crate. You can mantle onto a low platform nearby where some Gunpowder lies, then hop through the hole in the wall to reach Luiza's property.

Before going inside, note the outhouse on the right, and a locked shrine holding the Demon Crest by the gate you can't reach just yet.

Open the gate, and with the help of the villagers you'll be cautiously let inside. While you're told to wait in the front hall for a moment, take the time to save at the Typewriter, check the chair for the Dangerous Creatures File, and an interesting photo book on the opposite table.

When ready, head down the hall to meet the remaining survivors of the village. Of course, as expected in a Resident Evil game, friendly faces won't be around very long.

When things take a turn for the worse, you'll be attacked but saved by the girl from earlier, and led into a garage area. The truck works, but is missing its keys. Leave Elena behind and make your way into the next room - where a barricaded door is the only thing between you and freedom. Ethan will want to ram it with the truck, but you need those keys, so grab an Herb in a potted plant in the corner as you head left into the kitchen.

Most of the drawers here are empty, save a bottom drawer with some Lei, and the Truck Key to the left of the sink. A nearby note mentions there's something with the key, so inspect it to find a clasp to open and reveal a Screwdriver. Before you leave, search the back of the kitchen to find some Shotgun Ammo, then return to Elena and the truck.

Using the Truck Key, Ethan will try and bust out with limited success. You'll have to climb up to the rafters in the house towards the attic window - but unfortunately Elena won't be joining you.

After the cutscene ends, you can drop out of the window and back to the ground, grab some Chem Fluid in the nearby outhouse, and use your new Screwdriver to retrieve the Demon Crest.

Returning to the Fallow Field you'll witness a very shocking sight as a mysterious figure makes short work of the last remaining villager. Thankfully she'll disappear into the field, letting you return to the castle gate without incident.

Ignore the old crone and be sure to use the Save Point in the Church, then head to the gate and insert both the Maiden Crest and Demon Crest, and turn them until they face the right direction.

As you approach the small drawbridge, note that you can actually shoot the crows as you find them exposed, and can sometimes get some Lei for your trouble - if you wish.

Once you cross the drawbridge, you'll enter a small hallway leading to a sealed door, but as soon as you try to open it, you'll be waylaid by a very strange man with some very strange powers. It's time you got a face to face meeting with your real adversaries in Castle Dimitrescu.

Castle Dimitrescu

Meeting the Four Lords

As Ethan is subjected to a very interesting discussion between the "Lords" of this region on who gets to have some fun with him, the strange man named Heisenberg will be named the winner by their leader - Mother Miranda.

You won't have long to make sense of it all before Heisenberg starts his own version of The Running Man with you as the main attraction.

- Escape Heisenberg's Games

As soon as you drop into the pit, start sprinting down the corridor and evading the enemies appearing at the sides. When you reach a fork in the road, turn a hard left to avoid incoming Lycans, and interact with the wooden beams to create a path forward.

You'll have to drop down into a narrow platform over a pit, so keep moving forward and sprint past the archers until you are ambushed again and fall deeper into the caverns.

With barely enough time to recover from your fall, the spiked ceiling above you will start to come crashing down, so waste no time in moving to the wall in front of you to kick away the wooden planks and crouch into the next hallway.

Once you drop down into the next big room, things will get even more dire as spinning blades start coming for you - with no way to pass them. In order to survive, look back at the wall you just dropped down from, and one corner will have the smallest of alcoves to hide in as the blades draw close - but not close enough to kill you.

Once the trap breaks down, you'll be able to crawl through to the other side, and inspect two crates that were shredded to find some loot'. Move forward through several small rooms and corridors filled with inert traps - it seems they all think you're dead, as the place is deserted and devoid of enemies.

Finally, you'll reach a door to unlock that will take you right back to the room you first met Heisenberg, and you can now use the lever to open the way forward.

- Look for Rose in the Castle

Goat of Warding - As you explore the creepy vineyard outside, check along the walls near the "scarecrows" to spot a goat along the rocky outcroppings, and shoot it to break the bobbling trinket.

The small Vineyard has a few creepy scarecrows and a Herb, but not much else, so continue up to meet a very interesting merchant.

The Duke, as he's called, can provide services that include buying and selling a variety of items, as well as upgrading your weapons. You probably don't have too much Lei at this point, so it might be best either to just sell some treasure you've found, or buy the Shotgun Ammo recipe.

Castle Dimitrescu Entrance

Leave the Duke behind (you haven't seen the last of him), and enter the castle proper. You'll arrive in a modest entrance hall with a painting of three women, the daughters of Lady Dimitrescu. While you are no longer able to go back the way you came, you can start vandalizing the property in earnest.

Be sure to check the entrance hall for an urn you can break, and a cabinet with glass you can break to reach some Gunpowder. There's also a lift room to the right with some Lei on a table, but with the lift inoperative, head left instead and sneak a peek at the Guest Book File before moving through the door.

Most of the doors you pass here will be locked, forcing you on a narrow path - but at least you can break another urn. You'll be drawn into a great hall with a small staircase and some sort of door with an inscription.

However, before you can make sense of it all, the daughters of Lady Dimitrescu will introduce themselves - rather painfully - before taking you to their mother.

After the ensuing cutscene, you'll be left to hang around and wait for them to come back - which you should probably not do. As painful as it's going to be, you'll need to look up at your right hand and interact with it to free yourself, and finally get back on your feet. Thankfully, Ethan seems to be made of some pretty stern stuff.

Before you leave the bedchamber, pick up the Crimson Glass from a nearby table, and cautiously make your way back towards the Hall of the Four.

Note - Be on the lookout for such treasure as you continue to explore the areas around the village. These items can vary in where they are found, but will sell for a premium price to The Duke, and won't take up any extra space in your inventory. Some can even be combined to sell for much more than they would go for separately.

The door past the other room is locked, as is a nearby drawer, but to escape you can look towards a fireplace grate and crouch down to find a hidden passage beyond.

Grab some Rusted Scrap on the left as you enter the narrow crawl space, and move to the end of the hall to find a statue holding a Maroon Eye Ring, and the statue will pivot to reveal a secret passage back to the castle halls.

As you exit the secret passage, open a drawer opposite you to grab some Chem Fluid, and then turn to break a glass cabinet and gain a Crystal Fragment. The door to your left leads back to the hall you were abducted in, but you can also head back down the hall to unlock the doors to the bedchamber, and look for some Gunpowder in another drawer near the door.

In the Hall of the Four, it won't be long before four angel statues appear out of the ground with different markings where their heads should be - a puzzle that prevents you from leaving the castle, and you'll have to come back with the right tools later on. For now, take a look through the small door opposite where you came in to find the Merchant's Room, where The Duke has now taken up residence in a Safe Room.

You can buy or sell some extra wares, save, and also take note of the Labyrinth Puzzle in this room, and the nearby note, The Labyrinths File.

- Find Dimitrescu's Chambers

Your best bet of finding your daughter currently lies in Dimitrescu's room, but to get there you're going to need to search up and down this expansive castle.

Thankfully, the doors to the Main Hall have been unlocked, and you can now head up to the large room, and unlock the door leading back to the Entrance Hall.

Near the door to the entrance hall, look for a drawer containing Handgun Ammo, and an urn in the far corner to break. The door beyond is currently locked, so make your way up the stairs to the second level.

Head into the Wine Room and grab the Chem Fluid on the barrel, and check the main table for the Winemaking History File that mentions a valuable bottle adorned with silver flowers, much like the bottle stand at the end of the room.

Back in the upper Main Floor, look to the right for some urns you can break, and a locked door.

Moving to the other side of the upper floor, stop to look at a large portrait of a man with his hand extended. The top of the frame gleams - and you can shoot it to gain a Crystal Fragment.

Once you've broken the last urn, inspect the locked Prioress Door that's missing an eye. If you played the Maiden Demo, this will be very familiar. Look in your Key Items and inspect the Maroon Eye Ring, and examine it to gain the Maroon Eye, which you can then place in the door.

However, as soon as you enter, you'll be assaulted by one of Dimitrescu's daughters, who wants nothing more than to drain out all of your wonderful blood. Don't bother trying to run back to the Main Hall, and don't waste your bullets - they won't have any effect (besides slowing her down just a bit).

Instead, continue down the corridor you just unlocked. An insect swarm will prevent you from using the door again, so run down and take a quick left into a Dressing Room.

Before she can give chase, move to the back of the room and destroy the weak wall to find a secret passage with a pit - and jump in before the vampiress can reach you.

Castle Dimitrescu - Basement

In this underground passage, you'll be safe from her advances for the moment. As you move through the old room, look for a tray table with A Maid's Diary File you can read to get an important clue about Dimitresu's daughters.

Moving down the stairs, grab some Rusted Scrap from an alcove as you move closer to the music, and crouch down at the end to find a small hole leading to a room a certain lady of the castle just happens to be leaving, carrying what appears to be the silver-adorned bottle you need.

With Dimitrescu gone, look on a table near where you crawled out to get some Handgun Ammo, and move around the Tasting Room to the next set of stairs.

Note the ceiling as you enter the sloping hall - there's another glow in the ceiling you can shoot to get another Crystal Fragment.

Further into the Wine Cellar, crack open a nearby crate, and make your way into the Hall of War. What seems like a dead end is actually a puzzle, the clue to which can be found as you turn around. "Trust the light."

    Get to trusting with the light by moving into the hanging brazier to push it towards each of the pillars on the side. Push them all the way, and each will light up when it touches the hanging fire. Once both are lit, the way will be made clear.

    You'll be down in the prison now, which is eerily silent. Move through the first row of cells until you reach a blockade, and check on the right for a Treatment Candidates File. Head left through a cell with a broken wall to get around the barricade, and search the opposite cell for another letter, an Observation Report File.

    Once you reach the larger open room lined with cells and hanging body bags, you'll likely hear that you're not alone down here anymore. Before proceeding on, check each of the cells along the walls for crates to break'.

    Slowly enter the next hallway, and ready yourself, as three bloodless ghouls called the Moroaica will start shambling out to greet you. These enemies are slower than Lycans, but will often try to swarm you and swing some deadly looking weapons around.

    Slowly backpedal into the previous rooms as you aim for the head when possible. If they get too close, you can also shoot their arms and legs to disarm and stun them to get some breathing room, otherwise lead them on a chase through the wider previous room, and be prepared to block their strikes and shove them back when needed.

    Once the first group has fallen, head back into the hall and search the cell on the left for some Lei and move along the broken cell walls towards another crate - but watch for a hole in the wall at the end where another Moroaica will crawl out of - and unload on her before she gets up.

15

Grabbing the Pipe Bomb from the crate where the Moroaica crawled out of, see if you can get any use out of it as you move into the Chamber of Solace.

Move forward through the room quickly until you see several Moroaicas coming out of the cells to greet you - then backpedal and toss your pipe bomb to try and catch the entire group, and mop up the rest after the explosion!

Loot the corpses as they turn to dust - which should include a trinket from the Maiden Demo, Ingrid's Necklace, and grab some Shotgun Ammo on a nearby barrel before you move towards a hole in the ceiling, where another Moroaica or two should shamble out. You should have a lot more room to let them stumble towards you as you take some well placed headshots. Finally, search the cells on the right wall for Handgun Ammo and Rusted Scrap.

As you move into the next dungeon area, there's a mysterious locked door up ahead, but as you turn right you'll run into one of Dimitrescu's daughters. To escape, you'll need to quickly navigate the maze of bars and get around her to the exit.

Dimitrescu's Daughters - First Fight

Back up to let her come through the first gate, then run right to the far wall and through a broken wall back towards the middle. She'll likely try and ambush you here, so either duck past her, shoot to disperse her, or time a block and dart right again to the far wall, move left and take the stairs to get away.

The vampiric young lady will keep following you - so hurry past the items for now as you go up the stairs and to the right, and you'll find a weak wooden wall to interact with. Before you can get away, she'll launch you into the next room - but in the ensuing struggle her weakness will be realized.

With the extreme cold blowing in, she won't be able to dodge your bullets anymore, so take the opportunity to swap to your shotgun and unload a bunch of slugs into her face.

She may be slower now, but she can still fight, and will swing wildly with her sickle. You can try sidestepping her to strafe around the room, but if you get cornered, time your block to punch and force her back, and let off a few rounds while she's stunned.

There's more Handgun Ammo on a table on the side of the room, and on the shelf in the back. use them if you get low, and keep unloading shots until she finally starts to freeze in place, and eventually she'll shatter at your feet, leaving behind a Crystal Torso you can sell to The Duke.

One daughter down, two to go.

Note - Not only are breaking the windows a key component of making Dimitrescu's daughters vulnerable, there's also an achievement / trophy in it for you if you can break every window possible in the castle (you can tell they can be broken if they aren't covered by curtains). You can shoot the other window in this room to get started on this task.

If you escaped the basement rather quickly, you can head back now to find Chem Fluid on a barrel by the passage entrance, some Shotgun Ammo by the stairs down, as well as more ammo and Lei in the crates back in the maze.

Moving into the kitchen, be sure to grab the Sanguis Virginis from the bloody bowl, and then check a nearby cabinet for A Cook's Diary File.

Before leaving the kitchen, smash the crate, and check the fireplace for some Rusted Scrap.

The real prize waits in the next hall - you can spy a small briefcase on a table next to a locked drawer, and opening the briefcase reveals your first Weapon Mod, the LEMI Recoil Compensator!

As for the locked drawer, be sure to search the table along the hall for a Lockpick - though it's your choice if you want to unlock the drawer behind you for a Wooden Angel Statue you can sell for Lei, or head back to the bedchamber to unlock a drawer with Shotgun Ammo, just be sure to use it on one of them.

The Dining Room has a locked door leading to the Courtyard, but for now at least you can inspect the drawers on the far end for Gunpowder, and look carefully along the ceiling for a glowing spot to shoot and claim a Crystal Fragment.

Note - Even though you've defeated one, the other daughters of Dimitrescu will still haunt your footsteps from time to time, and may try to chase you in the areas around the Great Hall. Luckily, they move fairly slow, give up easily, and won't go into the Dining Room or similarly cold areas nearby, giving you lots of places to escape.

With the bottle of bloodwine in your hands, head back to the Main Hall and up toward the Tasting Room on the second floor, and place the Sanguis Virginis on its rightful stand to unlock a secret room that holds the Courtyard Key, as well as some Gunpowder.

Now would be a great time to head back to The Duke and save, sell the crystals and treasure's you've accumulated, and buy some upgrades for your weapons - you've still got a lot more to explore in the castle, and it's only going to get more dangerous!

Castle Dimitrescu - The Path to Dimitrescu's Chambers

Using the Courtyard Key, head through the Dining Room into the large expansive open area. It's a little too quiet, but thankfully there's no danger to speak of yet.

There's an urn to the left with loot', and one to the right as well. Searching the lower courtyard's railing, you can pick up a Herb among the foliage, and spy an urn on the far side of the courtyard.

There's also a small yellow birdcage hanging under the balcony on the south side of the courtyard you can shoot down for 1,000 Lei.

Since you can't go through the door on the left, take the far right door to trail after the ominous lady of the castle as she heads upstairs.

Once she's gone, open a drawer on the left for Chem Fluid, and then move up the stairs to break an urn.

As you move into the grand hallway, you'll hear Lady Dimitrescu raging behind a locked door, so you'll need to find another way to get over to her room.

Opposite her room is a map of the main part of the castle - showing you that there's a path to the Terrace to get behind her chambers, but the way won't be that straightforward.

The end of the hall leading to the Terrace is blocked (but you can break open a glass cabinet to get some Gunpowder, and spot some Handgun Ammo in a drawer earlier in the hall). Instead, head into the Hall of Ablution to encounter your next puzzle.

The Hall of Ablution features a pool of blood surrounded by four different statues facing one another. In order to solve this puzzle, you'll need to make the statues face a certain way - and the clue is in an engraving at the end of the room:

"Women are blind to male advances, but the poor shall take their chances to give their lord their bounty sown, so that soon the wine may flow."

Since the women are blind to male advances, make sure both the noblewoman and hooded woman holding the wine face each other. And with the poor giving their lord their bounty, turn the group of men towards the man on the horse. The rider should still be facing the hooded woman, thus completing the puzzle and draining the pool.

Goat of Warding - As you descend into the depths of the Distillery, look near the candles to spot another bobbling goat you can destroy.

Carefully make your way through the bloody waters and grab some Rusted Scrap before moving through the narrow corridors, and note the Moroaica falling into the waters before disappearing.

There's a crate nearby', and as you turn around to the next hallway, move slowly and you may notice small ripples emanating up ahead.

A Moroaica will pop out of the blood waters to grab at you, so quickly backpedal and unload into its face to put it down.

Moving into a larger area, one Moroaica will appear behind a line of barrels, while another will pop up down a corridor on the left. Try to take them out one at a time so you don't get flanked, and then grab some Handgun Ammo by a barricade, and move to the next hall.

Watch for another Moroaica to pop up in front of a crate you can break, and then slowly move through the corridor to spot another Moroaica after the hanging bodies that will come up to lunge at you. Before moving into the next room, look to the right for some Metal Scrap.

There's a larger distillery room here, and more Moroaicas will appear in the far corner

- making it a great opportunity to plant a mine for them all to trip on as they stumble forward.

Look behind some boxes in the corner for Gunpowder, and break the last crate here, and then move up the stairs at the end but watch out for one last Moroaica trying to ambush you, and break the crate behind it before climbing back up to the Terrace.

Up on the Terrace, look behind you for a Herb, and then check out the small room for a Save Point and some Lei under the piano.

When you're ready, cross the rickety balcony to eavesdrop on Lady Dimitrescu as she gets a call from her master - and note that she places a key under the candle holder. After she leaves the room, break a nearby urn on the balcony, and then head inside.

Rose is nowhere to be found, but you can at least check a sofa for Alcina Dimitrescu's Diary File, and grab Dimitrescu's Key from where she threw the vanity.

She's locked the door she left through - so use the key on the main door, only to get caught in the act.

Castle Dimitrescu - Dungeons

- Escape the Castle

Ethan will get thrown into the dungeons - literally. You'll need to find a way back up, so start winding through the passages and pick up some Gunpowder from a bucket next to the cell, and loot a crate near a hole leading out into the Dungeon.

The Dungeon is vast, full of twists and turns, and too empty to be trusted. Note the gates all over the place, and move to the back right to find a crate with a lot of loot', as well as Chem Fluid down nearby.

As you reach the first gate, you'll soon find that Lady Dimitrescu is tired of letting you do what you please - and you've really gotta hand it to her brash interruption.

In order to survive, you'll need to move as quickly as possible given the circumstances. Since you're very much wounded, you'll need to lure Lady Dimitrescu into charging forward before ducking into side passages to slip around past her.

She can deal incredible damage, and after extending her claws, she'll lunge forward - so be sure to duck around cover to put distance on her when she prepares for a lunge.

It's very important to note that opening the gate you were trying earlier will still take some time, and you likely can't just stand around waiting while Dimitrescu is on the rampage.

Let her chase you around the pillars until you spot the gate has fully opened, and then make a mad sprint to the end of the next corridor, down the stairs, and into the Hall of Sorrow.

Grab the Mask of Sorrow, one of the four puzzle pieces needed to escape the castle, and the platform will lift back up to the Courtyard.

Thankfully, now that you have some distance on Lady Dimitrescu, Ethan will be able to rearm himself as the lift goes up.

Finding the Mask of Joy

The Courtyard is now teeming with Moroaicas. There are a lot of them, so it's best not to stick around and let them beset you on all sides. It's better that you either quickly run off back to The Duke, or utilize Dimitrescu's Key to enter the door on the north side of the Courtyard.

You can also quickly run back to Dimitrescu's chambers and check her bathroom that was locked before to find a drawer with treasure - Lady's Lipstick.

Note - If you decide to return to The Duke he'll give some more words of encouragement, but you should expect to start encountering Lady Dimitrescu often now. Much like Jack Baker or Mr. X, Lady Dimitrescu will start wandering the halls of the castle in an attempt to rip you to pieces. Bullets have no effect on her (other than making her pause to shake it off every so often), and her lunging claw swipes have a deadly reach and deal a ton of damage.

Things can get even worse if one of her daughters also shows up, so be prepared to either use the side passages to get around the Main Hall, or beat a hasty retreat to the Merchant's Room where she won't follow, and wait until she wanders off.

Crossing the Courtyard, use Dimitrescu's Key to enter the foyer of the Opera Hall, and grab the Castle Map (Annex) from the wall across from you. The door downstairs is locked, so head up and break a glass cabinet at the top to grab some Gunpowder, then look in a nearby table for Handgun Ammo and the Grand Chambermaid's Notice File before you enter the Opera Hall.

As you enter the upper balcony area, you'll no doubt hear the noise of several Moroaicas lurking nearby. Pause for a moment and look at the ceiling above the small table here to shoot a shiny Crystal Fragment down to grab, then check the table at the far end to grab and inspect the Further Observations File.

Moving along the balcony, head left first into a small room where a Moroaica is waiting to grab you. After dispatching it, look near the disassembled labyrinth puzzle for a Flower Swords Ball, the item you need to interact with the labyrinth puzzle in the Merchant's Room.

Head back around the other side of the balcony and watch for more Moroaicas around the stairs going down, and note the locked drawer at the top of the stairs that holds Sniper Rifle Ammo. There's an urn at the bottom of the stairs, as well as Rusted Scrap in the fireplace, Gunpowder on a chair in the corner, and an Insect Observations Journal File on a small table.

Turn your attention to the piano for a small and easy puzzle. You need to match the piano keys to the sheet music displayed in order to solve the puzzle. If you don't read sheet music - not to worry, as pressing a key will show you how close you are to the actual note, and you need only go to the right to go higher, or left to go lower. Once you hit the right note, you'll move onto the next, so you don't have to get all the notes in one flawless string. Numbering the keys from left to right, the correct sequence is:

- 15, 12, 14, 13, 13, 16, 15, 16, 17, 17.

Completing the puzzle will unlock a small slot in the piano that holds the Iron Insignia Key, unlocking even more areas of the castle for you.

With the new key in hand, unlock the far door - but be wary should Lady Dimitrescu appear to try and pursue you, and double back the long way through the Opera Hall if you need to. She'll stop giving chase as you use the Iron Insignia Key on the Library Door - but only because someone else is waiting for you.

Dimitrescu's Daughters - Second Fight

Another of Dimitrescu's Daughters is waiting to slice you up in the Library, and there's no escape until you defeat her.

Ethan appears to be too polite to pull back the thick curtains on the windows in this room, but there is a massive skylight, and the key to her demise lies with it. Look around the center of the room's small wooden pillars near the far door to spot a small handle you can pull. Doing this will slowly open the skylight, letting all that frigid air into the room and leaving the daughter vulnerable to attack.

She'll likely panic when this happens, and start trying to run around the room to evade you, or alternate attacking you with her sickle if you get too close, so utilize the shotgun to interrupt her advances, and take shots from afar with the handgun when she runs.

Note that the skylight controls are timed, so keep an ear open to hear them slowly close again. As soon as the skylight closes, race back to the controls to open it once more and keep her vulnerable until she slowly stops moving and crystallizes, leaving another Crystal Torso. Two down.

There's plenty ammo here to grab if you need it, including Handgun Ammo in a back wall drawer, and on one of the shelves facing the center, and Shotgun Ammo on a shelf facing the wall.

Leaving the Library behind, you'll enter the Hall of Joy, which holds the second mask you need to get out of this castle - the Mask of Joy.

Now that you have the Flower Swords Ball, this is a good time to dip back to the Merchant's Room and try your hand at the Labyrinth Puzzle. It's a fairly straightforward game - tilt the large castle to roll the ball and try to land in the hole with the red flag.

You can do this by rolling the ball left and then down, then carefully to the right to cross the raising and lowering bridges. After rolling it up, slowly move to the left to avoid the several false holes in the middle - as long as you move slowly, you can have the ball hug the bottom lip to reach the hole with the red flag. This will reward you with a Crimson Skull, worth 8,000 Lei.

Finding the Mask of Pleasure

There's two more masks to find, and they can be done in either order - but there's a good reason to go after the Mask of Pleasure first.

Skirt around the Main Hall's upper floors to the south side where you escaped into the prison earlier - but this time use Dimitrescu's Key at the end of the long hallway.

You'll end up in the Hall of Pleasure, and the ladies won't follow you in. However, you won't be able to just walk away once you grab the Mask of Pleasure, as the door will seal unless something is adorning the statue.

Look around the room, and break an urn, and check a nearby drawer for a Silver Ring (but don't sell it as is just yet!).

There's also a sparkling Crystal Fragment on the ceiling you can shoot down.

Looking carefully, you can spot a hole in the fireplace you can crawl through that leads to a secret passageway with some Rusted Scrap on a shelf.

Dimitrescu's Daughters - Third Fight

The last of the three daughters will ambush you in the Armory, and there are no breakable windows or skylights to speak of - but there is a large crack in the wall coming from behind a shelf.

As soon as the fight begins, dart past the daughter to the shelf and pull it aside to spot a weak stone wall you need to open somehow.

Run to the far right table to find several Pipe Bombs, and quickly toss one at the crack with light coming through it. The blast will rupture the stone wall, letting all that wonderful cold air inside.

The fight will play out much the same as the others - in her vulnerable state, you can keep her from attacking with well-placed shotgun blasts, or get some distance and unload with your pistol - or even another Pipe Bomb if you find yourself low on ammo. There's also more Shotgun Ammo and Handgun Ammo on the barrels in the room.

She can still deal major damage, so be ready to block and push her back if she starts swinging, then backpedal and open fire until she begins to wildly swing around while crystallizing.

Finally, all three daughters will trouble you no more.

You still need a way out of the Hall of Pleasure, so look around and be sure to grab the

Lockpick where the Pipe Bombs were, then look up at the top of the wall to find a Mounted Animal Skull.

Grab it, and inspect the head to find a screw at the back you can take out, giving you the Animal Skull with the same four points as the Mask of Joy.

Replace it on the large sculpture, and you're free to go.

Finding the Mask of Rage

There's only one mask left, and you'll need to go to great heights to reach it. Return to the Main Hall and slink around back to the Hall of Joy, and then duck into the Atelier (Lady D won't follow you here, thankfully).

Inside you'll find Handgun Ammo in a large class cabinet, a very imposing portrait of Lady Dimitrescu, and another painting with five bells and a note, "Let the five bells of this chamber ring out". In order to proceed, you must find and strike each bell - a fire will light to confirm, and you can find them in the following locations:

- Just below the small staircase on a small table.
- On top of the large glass cabinet that held the ammo
- Swinging back and forth through the holes in the wall alongside the gears
- On top of the chandelier
- Through the skylight off in the distance in view from the balcony at the top of the short stairs

Once all five are struck, the large portrait will move aside, revealing a path forward.

As you enter the passage, look in an urn on the left to grab a Herb, then climb the long ladder into the Attic.

Goat of Warding - Once you enter the Attic, look around from where you came up to spy another bobbling Goat nearby behind the ladder among some boxes.

Continue through the abandoned room to find Gunpowder in a box on the right, and a Treasure Map next to a breakable crate.

Turning around, don't miss the prone body of a Moroaica lying in the corner, and take it out before it can rise up to fight. Grab the Lockpick she was guarding, then search the opposite side of the room for a table with the Rumors of a Dagger File, which may be the key to defeating the lady of the castle.

As you move to leave the Attic, don't miss the F2 Rifle on a chair at the end of the hall. You may have to do some inventory juggling to fit it in, and you may want to consider buying the inventory upgrade from The Duke to make things easier.

Out on the Rooftops, you'll witness several winged creatures called Samca taking flight around the area, before circling the spires or perching on ledges nearby. You can either try to snipe a few of them early, like on the one nearby that perches to the right, or wait for them to come to you.

These enemies are a lot like flying Moroaica, but they dart around much faster. They'll try to get you to waste ammo darting back and forth before flapping several times and swooping at you with their strange horn-like protrusions. However, even a few well-placed handgun shots can send them crashing to the ground, letting you either unload more bullets or slash them with a knife until they expire.

Be sure to check the sloping roof as you kill the first Samca, and you'll find an urn to break.

Further up you can find a Lift to take you back down to the Entrance Hall, creating a nice shortcut back down to the first floor. As you descend, look to the wall above the door leading out to spot a Crystal Fragment you can shoot down and collect.

Back up on the Rooftops, crack open the urns on the other side, and prepare for one or two Samcas to ambush you as you make your way along the outer roof. If multiple enemies show up at once, you can also wait until they dive close to take them out with a well-placed shotgun blast. Some may drop a Crystal Wing that you can sell for a nice profit.

Keep moving along the rooftops until you reach a dead end, then head up the slope and look for some Gunpowder on a ledge as you move to the middle.

As you move towards a small spire in the middle, left of the zipline, be sure to look above the small window to spot a small glowing Crystal Fragment you can shoot down and add to your collection. Cross over the sloped tiles into the inner rooftop to find an urn to destroy.

Two more Samcas wait in the spire above, but you can snipe one of them early as it perches on the top if you want. Break the urns in the Belfry, and then take the zipline over to the Tower of Rage.

In here, you can find the final mask, the Mask of Rage, and finally attempt to escape this place.

- Escape the Castle

You can try taking the lift down, but there's a good chance Lady Dimitrescu is waiting for you at the Entrance Hall, which may force you to quickly run back to the lift and go up, taking the longer way back through the Attic.

The Prison Treasure

Remember that you found a treasure map in the Attic that pointed to a locked door near the prisons where you killed your first daughter of Dimitrescu? Head back down that way, and take out any Moroaicas that now wander the dungeons until you reach the locked door, and open it using the Iron Insignia Key.

Inside is a puzzle similar to the other Prison puzzle, but this one can be a bit more annoying to deal with. There are two swinging braziers - both unlit, guarding a sarcophagus that you can't reach. In order to light the swinging braziers, look at a cracked wall near the back where a light source is emanating from. Search the nearby walls for a Pipe Bomb and blow open the wall to reveal a large torch.

The difficult part now is using the wonky physics of trying to push a swinging brazier in first person without being able to directly hold it. You can try and push them by running into them, but it's not recommended. If you want a much easier time, you can crouch down and fire a few well placed shots to send the brazier moving much quicker.

As long as you're accurate and don't mind wasting several bullets, you can light both the braziers this way - just remember both braziers will need to be swinging towards each other to light up, so you may need to stagger your pushes or shots. Luckily, there's Handgun Ammo both in an alcove and in a crate.

Completing the puzzle will unlock the sarcophagus for you, getting you the Azure Eye Treasure, that can be combined with the Silver Ring you found in the Hall of Pleasure to make the Azure Eye Ring, which sells for much more Lei. Be sure to also check the alcove where the standing torch is to find some extra Lei and a Crystal Fragment on a crate.

IMPORTANT - Make sure you have everything you need, and have explored the entire castle - and buy some upgrades from The Duke (including the inventory expansion if you haven't already) by selling all the treasure you've found so far. Once you leave, you won't be able to get back inside the castle, so leave no stone unturned if you care for being a completionist.

When you're ready, sneak back into the Hall of the Four (and make sure Lady Dimitresu's back is turned as you slowly place each mask on the angel busts to slowly open the exit to the castle. For reference:

- The Mask of Joy has one peg
- The Mask of Sorrow has two pegs
- The Mask of Hatred has three pegs
- The Mask of Pleasure has four pegs

Break the urns on your way out', as well as more urns on either side of the walkway outside.

As you enter the Tower of Worship, you'll find a lone sarcophagus that has the one item you need to level the playing field against Lady Dimitrescu - a poisoned dagger. Speaking of her...

Boss Fight - Lady Dimitrescu

You'll now have an exclusive look at Alcina Dimitrescu's true form, and it's not a pretty one. However, this state has left her vulnerable, specifically the humanoid form on top of the large winged creature.

In order to survive, you'll need to shoot carefully to hit her weak form on top, while dodging the lunging chompers of the terrifying beast below. To start, she'll leave you on a stairway up on the tower, but block your path. Get her to move away by aiming at her humanoid section with your pistol, and she'll eventually fly away.

Quickly run up the stairs and grab everything you see - the Sniper Rifle Ammo, First Aid Med, Shotgun Ammo, and Handgun Ammo.

As you move into the central tower, she'll land on the side and start slowly pursuing you in a circle around the tower. You'll want to take a few well placed shot at her upper body, then move back before the beast's jaws lunge at you.

It will always rear back for a moment before lunging forward, giving you the cue to turn and sprint away as it smashes through debris to get at you.

Look for the moments after its lunge when its wings move back to expose Dimitrescu to your shots, and either get close to the side for some shotgun blasts, or keep your distance while turning to let off some handgun shots before running away again.

After enough damage is dealt, Dimitrescu will take to the skies around the tower. Wait for her to start floating around in the air in a relative holding pattern, and she'll begin to summon an insect swarm. If not stopped, the swarm will eventually come to the tower and chase you, dealing damage over time unless you can outrun it. Instead, shut her down as soon as you see her begin this move by sniping her with your rifle, and she'll drop down after one or two hits.

After getting knocked out of the sky, wait for her to crash land back in the tower, and she might be dazed for a time, letting you get relatively close on either side of her and attack her vulnerable upper body.

After a few of these scenarios, she'll take the sky and then crash land on the tower again, dragging you into the middle as rubble falls all around you. Quickly run up the stairs to avoid her and her insect swarm before reaching the top of the spire. Before she follows, break the urns nearby to get some more ammo, and continue the fight.

In these close confines, you won't be able to run along the edges anymore. Instead, keep up the fire on her body, and strafe from side to side.

When you see the lower beast start to pulse red, move all the way to the right to dodge the lunge, then resume firing.

Utilize the shotgun after the lunge stuns her, and keep up the pressure until she starts to explode in a bloody mess, signaling the end of the fight.

When the scene ends, you'll be the proud owner of the Crystal Dimitrescu treasure, and nearby you can find a very mysterious Dirty Flask. It's time to leave the castle behind, and continue your search for Rose.

The Village (Second Visit)

The Path Back to the Village

Leaving the Tower of Worship behind after defeating Lady Dimitrescu, note the large drawbridge on the left that's been raised up.

Before moving forward, you can check out a small hut nearby and search the drawers for some Rusted Scrap, a Save Point, and a Craftsman's Note File that mentions a particular house.

Out the back window is a well, and an outhouse you can check for some free Gunpowder. To proceed, slash the locked gate with your knife to break the lock.

- Look for Rose

As you travel through a narrow passage, you'll enter a flooded tunnel with several fish swimming about.

You can actually kill these fish (crouch down quickly with your knife) and collect 3 Fish Meat - which can be traded with The Duke later on. Be warned, if you forget to kill these, you can't come back this way later - but there are more fish to find elsewhere.

At the end of the next hall, you'll meet the strange old crone again, who leaves an item in a chest, and motions to a mural of four different houses and lords, all surrounding some sort of pedestal with a familiar symbol...

When the crone leaves, open the chest to get the Winged Key, and use it to leave the cavern behind, and you'll come out onto the Ceremony Site.

It's quite a sight - with four large statues of four lords around a stone dias with that same striped symbol...

Off to the west, you can spy what looks to be a churning factory in the distance, but for now, head east back to the Village.

Look for a small path to the right to find some Sniper Rifle Ammo before heading down the foreboding stairs to a bridge across a river, where several Lycans lie in wait - many of them perched on the walls.

You can try and snipe one from a distance, and remember to wait for them to dart around before trying to pin them down with gunfire as they approach.

Goat of Warding - There's another Lycan down by the docks below you can get the drop on, and if you search the small dark room nearby, you'll find a noisy Goat of Warding to break.

Moving through the Lone Road, you'll spy a few open doorways on either side of the road.

The first opening on the right holds Rusted Scrap in the corner, while the opening on the left holds a Lycan guarding a crate.

Make a note of the last opening on the right, as there's a small chest in there that needs a key you don't have.

When you reach the Village's Altar, The Duke will appear, and shed more light on your predicament, as well as the fate of your daughter. It ain't great.

Reach the Red Chimney House

After you get somewhat of an explanation, be sure to check The Duke's wares for new items like recipes to make Pipe Bombs, and use the Save Point nearby. You don't have to deposit the flask at the Altar yet if you don't want to, and currently your key only has two wings, and cannot open the other doors that surround you.

Use the Winged Key to make your way back to the Village square. It's important to note that since your last visit in the morning, a few things have changed now that the time of day has shifted.

For starters, there are several bodies in the street now, and the drawbridge back to Castle Dimitrescu has been raised - but you can take the opportunity to kill the fish swimming in the moat to get 3 Fish Meat.

Just be wary, as a few Lycans will appear to feast on the bodies when you turn back from the castle. If you still have a Lockpick, you can return to the first house by the Maiden of War where you had met the old crone to unlock a drawer with several Shotgun Ammo.

If you head over to the Church nearby, you'll find that someone has set up a basecamp here and is following your progress - it seems the team that initially abducted your daughter have finally tracked down your location. Read the Church Computer File for more info.

Behind the church is a small graveyard you can now open with the Iron Insignia Key, leading to a small area with a few mausoleums, and several chickens you can gut to get 3 Poultry.

Be sure to stop back The Duke later to learn how you can give him meat to permanently upgrade your health and other abilities.

Goat of Warding - Be sure to look around the graveyard for a Herb, a crate to break, and a Goat of Warding behind one of the mausoleums in the back.

The Fallow Plot has also been altered with the burned bodies from Luiza's House now strung up as scarecrows, and several winged Samcas circle the field.

There's some items now by the house, but as they include ammo for weapons you don't have, leave the place for later.

The red chimney house is beyond the sealed green gate by the Maiden of War statue, but a nearby tractor has been moved to allow access to a nearby large house.

Enter into the basement at the front of the house to find Vivianite under the clay oven, and search the room for a Teddy Bear, Gunpowder, Lei, Rusted Scrap, and Chem Fluid.

Head around the back of the house to find a bloody barn area and a locked door, then turn back to go up the stairs to the main rooms where you can find Handgun Ammo in a cabinet, a locked drawer you can lockpick to get Shotgun Ammo, as well as Leonardo's Message File on the table.

As you move through the house, you'll hear a lot of commotion outside, and a room at the back has a door to the other side of the yard - as well as a Wooden Animal (Body) treasure you can combine with something else later on.

Move down and unlock the other yard door before going into the small barn where you can push aside a barricade - but be ready for a Lycan on the other side.

You're back in West Old Town now, and a nearby tractor is now blocking you from getting back onto the road leading to the red chimney house.

Take the path up to the large gate with the lock, and slash it to open a path to the Workshop. There's some Lei and Rusted Scrap out in the open here, and heading inside, you can find a large locked cabinet with a combination lock.

Thankfully, the combination code is not far away, just look nearby for a small photo of a man with some strange object grafted onto his back, and flip the photo over for a clue.

Looking out the window, you'll see three sets of numbers come into focus to reveal the code: 070408 . Just be prepared for a quick surprise, and then deal with the arrival.

Unlocking the cabinet will reveal a new gun, the M1911 Handgun as well as a Jack Handle for the tractor.

Note - now that you have a new handgun, you may want to consider selling the old one - but it might be worth it to make sure you empty the clip on some enemies first because you won't be getting those bullets back if you do! You can also hang onto it, as both can be continually upgraded by The Duke as the story progresses.

Leaving the Workshop, several Lycans are waiting for you, which seems like a good time to test out your new weapon - and make use of its fully automatic ability to hold down the trigger to unload on the group. If things get dicey, you may want to consider using a Pipe Bomb or Mine to even the odds of them trying to swarm you.

When the group goes down, head back to the tractor and use the Jack Handle to get under the vehicle and back onto the main road. Looking behind you, the first house at the edge of the village is missing its dead horse, which has been replaced by a crate to break.

You can also now unlock the drawer in the home with a lockpick to get Sniper Rifle Ammo. However, if you investigate the barn on the side of the house, you'll encounter a pig that can be killed for its 2 Meat.

Remember also the barn in the back that had a yellow hanging birdcage. Now that you have a gun this time around, shoot it down to grab some Shotgun Ammo.

Down the road toward the red chimney house, there's two Lycans waiting by a tractor - try to snipe the one on top to explode its head, then kill its friend who comes charging up at you. Moving past them, there's a few more up the street you'll need to contend with, but let them come to you, and try using your shotgun when they bunch up in the tight corridor. Before going down the street, note the cart that has been pushed further toward the village square, revealing a small hole in a hut near the red chimney house. You can't reach it from here, but the hut does have a Pipe Bomb in it.

You may also want to have it ready, as moving down the narrow road will reveal a new enemy - the Armored Lycan. Covered with sharp and deadly metal pits, this armored foe is very tough, if a bit slow to advance, and you're going to want to keep your distance against his savage multiple strikes.

Toss a Pipe Bomb and aim at his helmet and chest plate to break away the armor, and then fire off your rifle to deal major damage to his exposed parts. Keep backpedaling away and don't let him get close so you can keep shooting from a distance until it falls. You'll likely be rewarded for your efforts with a Perfect Crystal Skull that sells for a ton.

You can't re-enter the home you met your first survivor in, but you can finally cut the padlock on the home across the lane with the note on it. There's a Note on Luthier's House File on the front door from Beneviento's Gardener, who apparently holds the key to this home.

Still, you can check next to the house for a crate, and the small shack nearby where a Lycan is hiding, along with some Gunpowder, Handgun Ammo, and a Madalina (Body) treasure. Be sure to also check the outhouse here to find a Lockpick.

Goat of Warding - Look between Luthier's house and the shack to find a small area, and on top of a firewood pile you can find another goat to shoot.

Using the Iron Insignia key on the gate near the large house on the street, as it leads to a ladder to cross to the red chimney house.

Be sure to enter the small shack first to find Lei and a Water Wheel. With this key item, you can now raise up all the wells around the village to collect various items!

Climbing up the ladder next to the shack, you can collect some Metal Scrap along the way, then finally drop down into the yard of the red chimney house.

There's a few chickens scurrying about that you can kill for 2 Poultry Meat, some Gunpowder on a stove outside, and you can unlock the gate to the Maiden of War, and the door where you got the Pipe Bomb. Be sure to also look for an outhouse that holds a Large Crystal.

With the front door locked, go around the back to find a ladder to the roof, and drop inside.

Unfortunately it seems the man of the house is either gone, dead, or he's the Lycan currently eating a woman in the other room. Regardless of which, kill the beast, and open the nearby cabinet for Handgun Ammo.

This won't be a total waste of time, as the nearby kitchen table holds Eugen's Diary

File, and a box with a note about how the Winged Key can be upgraded - and just so happens to have the parts to make it a Four Winged Key!

- Return to the Duke

With this new information in hand, it's time to return to The Duke to learn of your next objective. Before you go however, you may want to take another quick lap around the Village to use the water wheel at various wells:

- The well to the right of the Maiden of War statue holds the Wooden Animal (Head) Treasure that can be combined with the Wooden Animal (Body) to sell for greater profit.
- The well behind the Church holds a Necklace with Two Holes that seems to have room 2 gems.
- The well behind the first house in West Old Town has one Lockpick.
- The well next to Luiza's House has 3 Pipebombs

When you're ready to get your next objective from The Duke, return to the Altar to learn that you'll need all four flasks to get your daughter back. Each flask is held by one of the "four lords" Mother Miranda controls, and you'll need to hunt each of them down in their lairs as you did with Lady Dimitrescu.

The Duke will update your map with the locations of the lords - as well as the locations of several treasure items you can keep an eye out for as you travel and return to previously explored areas. Be sure to also take the time to buy any more upgrades for your new weapons, and enhance your abilities with any food you hunt down.

With your winged key now upgraded to four wings, you have but one target you can pursue next, Donna Beneviento, the creepy doll maker of House Beneviento. Head north from the Altar to proceed into her domain.

House Beneviento

The Garden Path

Moving up the path from the Altar with your new Four-Winged Key, you'll enter a very eerie and fog-filled ravine, which is about to become even creepier when you notice all the hanging dolls.

The area is devoid of enemies, but you can snipe a crow or two to get some Lei from them.

The Path to House Beneviento

Goat of Warding - As you reach the incredibly nerve-wracking suspension bridge, fear not, it will hold. More importantly, if you look to the left at another bridge, you can spy a Goat of Warding to snipe from your location before crossing the bridge.

Making your way to the Garden, Ethan will begin to see visions - but if they are real or all in his head will be hard to say. Listen to the visions as you progress down the narrow path, as you won't be able to deviate right now.

You'll end up in a large gravesite with a large headstone for a member of the Beneviento family, but part of the slab with their name is missing. This site also holds a treasure, but you won't be able to access it just yet.

Move around to the back of the gravesite to find a large door with a slot, and a plaque next to it that reads "Give up your memories". You only have one real memory to part with at this point - it's an item you've carried with you from the start: The Family Photo.

Deposit it in the slot, and the door will open.

At this point the path behind you will seal, forcing you onwards to a lift to take you up and out to a path leading to a majestic - yet creepy - sight: House Beneviento, precariously perched on a cliff in front of a huge crashing waterfall. The entrance is covered in flowers, but devoid of any occupants.

Goat of Warding - Before entering, you can search the cliffside to find a small set of stairs to overlook the waterfall, and there's another Goat of Warding just behind the fence you can break. When you're ready, head inside the estate.

House Beneviento

Inside, the house is just as eerily empty as the path leading to it. The hall to the right of the Foyer is locked, and the stairs up include a very disturbing portrait of Donna and her puppet.

However, upstairs you'll find nothing out of the ordinary, and even the Living Room has nothing of note beyond a single picture on the table that depicts the same flowers growing outside the house.

Head down the hall past the Living Room until you reach a lift to take you downstairs to an equally confusing and empty hallway. The door on the left holds a Study with a projection room, and the long hallway will take you down to the Doll Workshop.

Here you'll find that creepy doll Angie holding the second flask you need, but if it seems too good to be true, it probably is. Before you can take it, the lights will go out, and Angie and the body on the nearby table will disappear - along will all your weapons and items!

- Escape House Beneviento

When the lights flicker back on, the body will be replaced by a doll that looks a little too familiar. The door behind you is now sealed with a combination lock, another nearby door seems to require a slender key, and the far door at the back of the workshop has two symbols, but is missing a third.

To get things moving, make use of the Save Point nearby, and then inspect the Mia Doll (and the photograph). There are many parts to the doll you can interact with, let's take them in turn:

- The doll's right hand and lower arm can be slowly removed, and looking at its base will reveal a symbol that corresponds to the far sealed door.
- The doll's upper right shoulder can be removed to find a Silver Key.

- The doll's left hand has a Blood Covered Ring that can be removed, and inspecting it shows some numbers - but not enough to use in the combination lock.
- The doll's left leg can be taken off to reveal a Winding Key in the knee area.
- The doll's chest is covered in bandages, but you lack the tools to cut it open.
- The doll's left eye can be moved to reveal an image of a crow in flight with a triangle - the second of three symbols needed for the far sealed door.
- The doll's mouth can be opened to reveal a strip of film, but it cannot be grasped without the right tool.

With the Silver Key, move to the corresponding locked door and open it to enter a Medicine Room.

The other door here is locked, but you can use the sink to wash the blood from the ring and turn it into the Wedding Ring.

Inspecting it now will reveal the full set of numbers: 052911, which you can then put into the combination lock and start moving back down the hall.

As you approach, a door that was previously closed will open slightly, so humor the ghosts down here and enter the Storage Room.

Inside the room, you can find a note from Mia about the music box that was in your home at the start of the game. However, it seems to be broken now, but you can use the Winding Key to open it up.

There are deep scratch marks all over the different parts of the interior of the music box, and you need to re-arrange them so that the longer gashes connect at the right parts. Numbering the different slots as you see them to start with, here's how the finished version should look:

- 1, 2, 3, 4, 5
- 2, 4, 1, 5, 3

Completing the puzzle correctly will earn you the Tweezers, so head back to the Mia doll and open her mouth to extract the Film.

Now you can head back up the hall to the Study by the Lift, and note the nearby breaker box now has a red light, but is locked. Inside the Study, examine the note, and the sets of film that you add yours to, and put them in the correct order:

- Rose's best friend in the whole wide world - 3
- She really likes this fairytale - 4
- The most important thing in the world to us - 1
- A wedding gift from grandma - 5
- Proof of Ethan's everlasting love for me - 2

With the correct order set up, play the movie to see… something entirely different. A well? Your next clue, it seems. As the film concludes, the screen will fall, and a bookcase will slide open to reveal a secret path.

Enter the creepy doll corridor and look for one holding Scissors that you can add to your key items, and then cut away the bandages in the wall to crawl forward.

You'll find a telephone here, and of course the moment you try to walk past it, the phone will ring, so answer it!

After the phone call ends, move down the hall and note the door with the engraving of a mother missing its child. Continue down to end up back in the Doll Workshop just as a figure moves out of the room. Enter the room and use the Scissors on the Mia doll to open up the chest and claim the Brass Medallion.

With this object, refresh your memory on the icon in the doll's left eye, and the three closed eyes on the doll's right hand, then head to the far sealed door. Place the medallion in the top right, then interact with the other two to get the correct symbols and the door will open.

You'll now enter the scene from the movie that was playing earlier, so head down the creepy stairs to the well, and climb in to reach the bottom. One of the doll hands here holds the Breaker Box Key - a way out of this hell may finally be in sight.

Getting out of the well, the nearby baby cradle has been smashed, as you return to the Doll Workshop, things are getting more unsettling. The Mia doll is missing, and a long blood trail seems to be extending into the hallway… Better use that Save Point now.

Sure enough, as you begin to make your way through the darkened hallway back to the breaker box, something will start moving out of the shadows toward you. Something very large, disturbing, and dangerous. Quickly turn and flee back to the Doll Workshop, where you'll need to make a judgement call.

If you're feeling confident in your ability to maneuver, you can use the table to wait on the other side until the abomination tries to move around to get you, then take the opposite side and sprint back to the breaker box.

If you'd rather play it safe, run into the Medicine Room and look for a large cabinet you can walk into and close behind you, staying out of sight as the abomination slowly searches the room for you. When it leaves, it should eventually disappear altogether, letting you reach the breaker box in relative safety.

Open the breaker box, and instead of a fuse you'll find the Relief of a Child.

You can use this by traveling back through the Study and out into the hall beyond, where that creepy doll sits just next to the Mother's Door.

Head through the door and down to a lower hallway, noting the bookcases that have blocked the next passage.

Make your way through the Kitchen to get to the other side of the hall to enter a bedroom. It's probably worth noting that you can interact with the bed to climb under it... you might see where this is going.

At the end of the bedroom next to a large cabinet, grab the Fuse and make your way back, only for that cursed abomination to appear at the top of the stairs after you leave the Kitchen. Quickly spring back to the bedroom and dive under the bed or into the large cabinet and wait things out as it slowly moves around to look for you. Be patient, and wait until it finally leaves and heads back up the hall before getting out, and it should vanish on its own.

The thing knocked over some bookcases outside the Mother's Door, so you'll have to take the long detour back through the Doll Workshop (and save once more if you need to), and then go back to the lift.

As you might expect, putting the fuse box in will trigger the wrath of the abomination, and it will take a few minutes for the lift to come back down. Don't waste any time, and quickly duck into the Study, and put the big table between you and the abomination.

When it finally moves in, let it try to move around to come towards you, then quickly sprint up the other side, out of the Study and open the lift door as fast as possible to be free of this hell.

Back on the ground floor of the House Beneviento, you'll hear another type of giggling - the cursed doll called Angie. Apparently, your time in hell isn't over yet.

Boss Fight - Angie

The house is now covered with creepy dolls on every floor, table, and wall, all of which seem to be controlled by Donna and her main partner Angie.

This boss fight is less of a true battle and more of a deadly game of hide and seek. Angie will attempt to hide in this part of the house among the many dolls, and if you take too long to find her, she'll summon a horde of them to try and tear you to pieces. Since you lack defensive measures or health options, you won't be able to last for long, so speed is the top priority.

The places in which Angie hides seems to be partially random, but she generally begins by hiding up on the second floor Guest Room, to the left of the bed. Look for the all white doll, and grab her to stab it with your Scissors.

When she flees again, head back downstairs, and look in the Living Room, as she is usually either behind the far desk, or in the side area with the large couch - and you can sometimes hear her making noises when you're close.

Note - When in doubt, follow the blood trails she leaves behind!

After stabbing her a second time, she should move into the Foyer, down the hall in front of the blocked door to the right of the front door. If she's not there, check the opposite hall and go to where the lift is to look for her.

Grab her one final time, and Ethan will put an end to both Angie and Donna Beneviento.

This will net you the next part of the Winged Key - examine the middle to form the Four-Winged Unborn Key. You should also grab the Legs Flask by the door, and inspect Donna's body to pick up the Angie Treasure, which you should sell to The Duke as soon as possible.

Return to The Village

Since there's nothing left of value to pillage or inspect in the house, leave it behind and start making your way back to the lift to head back to the Garden.

Moving past the large gravesite, you'll see things have now changed - perhaps you were seeing one too many illusions. The hanging dolls are in fact hanging bodies, and means you may have to deal with some enemies before long.

Sure enough, a fallen tree blocks the road back, forcing you to make a detour past an old shack. Break the nearby crate', and get ready to deal with Moroaicas. Some are draped over the gazebos, but they'll instantly come to life if you try to enter the Shack.

Lucky for you, the shack makes a good temporary fortress, as you can move a barricade over the door, and look to the left to find a W870 TAC Shotgun to add to your arsenal. Using your newfound weapon, fire through the barricade once they make a hole, and take out the horde as they try to break it down.

If they manage to succeed, reward their efforts by tossing a Pipe Bomb (or the Mine in the nearby crate) to scatter them, then exit and get some distance to pick off the rest with a rifle or handgun, otherwise you run the risk of getting swarmed in the shack.

Once the threat is over, make sure you grab the Lockpick from the shack, and Handgun Ammo from the nearby lean-to. If you head through the covered walkway to the back of the garden, you can find a large tree with a yellow birdcage hanging from it, and collect a bunch of Lei from the cage.

Around the other side of the tree, there's a small tombstone with a box you can open to find a Sun and Moon Ball much like the one for the Labyrinth puzzle in the castle.

Speaking of which, you can now head up through a nearby gate on the left to reach the Gardener's House (the same gardener who left a note about the locked house in the Village).

Outside his home there's a crate, and a well you can use the Well Wheel on to find a Madalina (Head) treasure, which combined with the body will offer quite a reward. You should also check the outhouse for a Photo of a Strange Bird.

Inside the house is a Save Point, Luthier's Key to the village house, a Gardener's Diary File by the bed, and some Explosive Rounds for a weapon you don't have yet - so whether you want to make room in your inventory or come back later is up to you.

Of course the most important thing in this home is the next Labyrinth Puzzle, which you now have the ball to play with. Using the Sun and Moon Ball, try to get the ball to the goal at the end.

It's a bit more simplistic than the castle's Labyrinth, as you need only navigate some winding slopes. However, the edges can easily send your ball flying off on the turns, so you'll either need to time it right when some of the fences raise up, or tilt back against the slope to move slowly and carefully from right to left and back again to the end goal.

Completing this puzzle will earn you the Onyx Skull, which is worth a ton to The Duke! Moving out of the Garden to the Suspension Bridge, you may spy several winged creatures flying along the river, but they won't bother you. However, moving into Potter's Field, there are more hanging bodies, which means more Moroaicas waiting for you.

One should fall down and rise to attack early, and from here you can either go quickly up the left path to find a Large Crystal on a tombstone next to a crate and a lone Moroaica coming out of the ground, or take the lower road where 2-3 more Moroaicas will come attack you. Note that there are also some flour bags on the high road you can use to blind them as they approach.

After defeating the Moroaicas, be sure to check around the lower path with the big tree for threel hanging birdcages (listen for the sounds they make twisting in the wind).

They each contain a good amount of Lei, and one of the nearby tombstones has Vivianite embedded in it. With all that loot gained, it's time for a quick pitstop back in the Village before moving off to your next Lord.

The Village (Third Visit)

The Maestro's Collection

While not much has changed since your earlier visit to the Village (except a few Moroaicas that have taken up residence in the graveyard), there are a few notable points of interest to check back in on, plus the area leading to the next lord.

Now that you have obtained the key from the Gardener's shack, you can now return to West Old Town and unlock the door using Luthier's Key.

Inside, look under the sink for Handgun Ammo, and a drawer in the other room for Chem Fluid, and a crate.

Above the crate, there's a lute hanging from the ceiling with a Yellow Quartz embedded in it, which you can smack to free.

The main treasure here is located in a cabinet with a combination lock, so you'll need to look around for clues.

There's a paper with the model number of a violin - but ignore that and instead look on the same table for a scrap of paper that says "I will never forget her fifth birthday".

Head to the kitchen and look in the corner to spot a small happy birthday drawing with a date on it: 27, 09, 17.

Input it into the combination lock, and you'll find both a Steel Hraesvelgr treasure, and a chest with an F2 Rifle - High-Capacity Mag you can combine into your rifle!

Luiza's Heirloom

If you haven't already, now will be a great time to return to the Fallow Plot to see what's become of Luiza's house.

Three winged Samcas circle the place, so you may want to snipe a few before they reach you. Another hides in the tall grass, so be sure to advance cautiously and avoid their lunges from the air.

Luiza's house is still a smoking wreck, but items have been placed around the entrance, including Luiza's Heirloom in a small box.

You can also find plenty of Handgun Ammo, some Explosive Rounds (which you'll find the weapon for soon), and some Magnum Ammo that you may want to leave until you find the Magnum later.

On the way out, pass through the tiny shack where you first met the girl and her father and jump through the window in the back to find a white pig you can kill for Quality Meat. If you haven't already, you can also use the Water Wheel on the well to get 3 Pipe Bombs.

Be sure to also check the small path below that leads to a dead end, and a few Chickens to get some Poultry and Rusted Scrap.

Be sure to carefully inspect Luiza's Heirloom in your menu. As it turns out, you can interact with the necklace to remove the Necklace Stone to sell for a good bit of cash. Even more important is inspecting the remaining necklace to find Luiza's Key hidden inside.

This can be used to finally unlock a small chest in the room back on the Lone Path outside the Altar, which contains Cesare's Goblet, a most valuable treasure to sell.

East Old Town

With the newly upgraded Winged Key, it's time to finally head back to East Old Town where you got attacked by that giant Lycan with the hammer.

He's not around anymore, but unfortunately, a new enemy is, and wastes no time practically mauling Ethan to death.

The werewolf beast known as the Varcolac is a terrifying foe, and can deal major damage quickly, so you'll need to run and gun and do your best to focus on surprise attacks before retreating into buildings.

The fight will start as it tosses you into the building, and as long as you keep some distance, you'll find it can't actually enter (but will swipe wide into the rooms you hide in), so either unload with the shotgun, or quickly climb to the roof as it loses track of you.

There's also a dead body in the building holding Vasile's Final Testament File, which mentions getting to the nearby watermill.

Big impact weapons like the Rifle and Shotgun work well here for damage, as will Pipe Bombs and Mines - but it can be hard to stagger.

However, if it does loose track of you and starts wandering away to the south, you may want to quickly drop down and run to the edge of the stream where a locked door can finally be opened with the Iron Insignia Key.

Inside is the GM 79 Grenade Launcher, a weapon that can launch explosive projectiles - ammo you may already have a few of by this point.

You should also break the nearby crate, and a Lockpick on a windowsill before leaving.

Using the launcher, fire off a few explosive rounds and finish up with rifle or shotgun blasts.

If your attacks don't kill it, the Varcolac may sometimes run around a corner into the far yard, only to leap over a nearby wall to try and ambush you.

Don't be afraid to run back into houses if you miss your shots or the beast begins to charge.

Just be sure to keep up the blasting and the beast should finally fall after a time, leaving behind a highly prized Crystal Beast.

With the major threat gone, you should still be on guard, as two Lycans are still hiding in the large barn where the radio was located, and may try to ambush you if you aren't ready.

The green slimy path along the river will take you to the next Lord, but there is one last optional treasure to hunt down - but it comes with a formidable foe.

Beneviento's Treasure

For this optional treasure, you're going to want to make sure you have a lot of ammo, especially explosive types, and a few First Aid Med, as the treasure won't be given up without a fight.

Head to the Village's graveyard above the Maiden of War statue, and you'll find along with some new ghouls, a small mausoleum has opened, allowing you to pick up a Broken Slab. This is the same slab that was missing from the large Beneviento tombstone past the garden.

While you're here, you may remember the Photo of a Strange Bird you got in the Gardener's outhouse, depicting a bright blue bird in a tree. This tree happens to be right next to the mausoleum, so take careful aim and dispatch it to get some Juicy Game.

Head back down the path toward the Beneviento House through the garden, and be sure to kill the large black goat by the shack to get 2 Meat.

When you reach the large tombstone, be ready. A giant wielding an even more giant axe will crash into the area signaling a miniboss fight. This large hulking enemy can deal a ton of damage with just a single swing, so you'll want to be ready to dodge at a moment's notice.

Beyond his slow and powerful overhead swings, this giant can and will leap across the entire arena if you put too much distance between you.

If the giant moves his weapon back into a stance, you'll need to be careful. It will either be a low stance with his weapon behind him, or holding his axe high. Either method will have the giant slowly advance upon you, and if it closes the distance, the giant will unleash a large sweeping strike that will deal major damage.

If that wasn't bad enough, the giant will also summon a few Moroaicas from time to time to help him during the fight. Depending on your ammo count, you may want to consider dodging around them as they move fairly slowly - but it's better to employ explosives to damage all of them when they move close together, so the Moroaicas can go down while you damage the giant. Luckily, the Moroaicas tend to drop lots of crafting resources, allowing you to stay in the fight longer by making more healing items or ammo.

Try to aim for the head after the giant swings or jumps and stays vulnerable for a bit, but always be ready to sprint away at a moment's notice. It will take a lot of firepower to bring it down, so if you're having trouble, you may want to come back later.

Should you defeat the giant, you'll gain a Giant Crystal Axe that sells for a huge amount, and if that wasn't enough, you can now put the Broken Slab at the foot of the tombstone, and it will reveal Berengario's Chalice which also sells for a huge amount. More than likely, you may want to use some of your newfound funds to buy some ammo back that you used to defeat the giant.

The Reservoir

Path to the Reservoir

Leaving the East Old Town behind, you'll find the gate has now been replaced by a wall of giant green goo - but luckily it can be broken apart with just a few handgun shots or a few more knife slices if you want to conserve ammo.

You'll end up outside a windmill, but the nearby gate is locked. Instead, attack the wall of goo to the right to find part of a ladder you can climb up and over into the yard.

Be sure to chase down and slaughter the two pigs for 4 Meat.

Make note of the Labyrinth puzzle outside, then head into the windmill and check the barrel on the right for a Photo of a Rare Animal that depicts a white pig you probably already killed near Luiza's House.

The Reservoir Mine

Take the stairs down to the lift that leads to the reservoir entrance, an old wet and rust mine. There's several locked doors down here, and a path leading to the left.

Be sure to look up as you take the left path, and shoot down a glowing spot for a Crystal Fragment.

Following the path upstairs, you'll be able to wedge yourself into a small alcove looking into Moreau's room, where he's busy watching static on TV with the Arms Flask right in front of you. The weird fishman will plead with you not to take it, and then begin to summon walls of goo to pen you in.

Quickly break it away and head back do the mine, only to find the way back is sealed off.

- Escape Moreau

Another gate has been ripped apart, leading to an exit out onto the Reservoir itself. Take in the sights, then make your way down to another windmill and a boathouse. There's a barrel on the left with and a chest on a boat out of reach.

Inside the boathouse you'll find The Reservoir and Giant Fish File alerting you that the key you need for the boat is back in the mine.

Head back into the mine and up some stairs on the left. On the right is some Handgun Ammo, and going left will lead to a gap in the boardwalk, but you can create a path by hitting the yellow supports to cause wooden planks to fall down.

Drop down a small ladder and look below for a crate, and then cautiously advance into the next large area. You might spot a Lycan wandering above with a torch who will drop down next to another Lycan feeding on something by a large tree.

See if you can ambush one to kill it quickly with a headshot and then defeat the second, and look around the grounds for a Herb. Be sure to also check the water's edge for Handgun Ammo in a boat, a barrel, and another barrel by the shack.

As soon as you move inside to grab the Boat Key, several Lycans will show up, including an Armored Lycan who jumps down from above. If you are quick and quiet, you can barricade the entrance and sneak out the back before they notice you. From here you can sneak out the back, and move left to spot several Lycans huddled near that makes perfect target practice for a Pipe Bomb or explosive round when the Armored Lycan moves near.

Two explosives should kill the bulk of them, at which point you should retreat to the water's edge where flour bags are.

Use them to blind the Armored Lycan before you follow up with a shotgun to his hopefully exposed head. If you are low on ammo, you can also try and sprint back to the ladder, as the Lycans won't follow.

Return back to the boathouse but be ready to deal with two Lycans hanging around the area. With the Boat Key in your possession, start things up and take the boat through the nearby cave entrance.

On the other side, a large fish-like creature will splash past you, but debris in the submerged fishing village will prevent you from going forwards.

Instead, head into another watery cave to dock, and move up to find a strange lab-like area - but before approach the green tarp, head right instead up a cave path and along a flowing stream.

Here you can find a pool of water where you can carefully search the shallow water for two catfish you can dice up to claim 4 Fish Meat. Look around the right walls of the cave and you can also shoot loose a Large Crystal on the wall.

Head back to the lab area beyond the green tarp to get reacquainted with a familiar face, but your reunion will get cut short by the arrival of the giant fish, who soon turns out to be a very disgusting and even more mutated Moreau.

Draining the Reservoir

When he dives back into the reservoir, he'll start to destroy the shaky platforms you're on, so quickly run away and jump to safer ground. He mentioned the exit is now underwater, so you'll need to find a way to lower the water level in the reservoir.

Luckily, you can drop down and investigate a nearby gatehouse to find a control panel for opening the sluice gates. Unfortunately, the station isn't powered because all the windmills aren't operating currently. Read the large poster on the wall to see the instructions, and note the colored paper by the console.

Be sure to explore the rest of the gatehouse to find your old pal The Duke, and a Save Point.

Make any upgrades and give the meat you found, then leave and check a nearby outhouse for some Chem Fluid.

Move along the pathway until you reach a fork with an old truck, and read the Changing the Cranks File on the driver seat.

To the right is an enclosure with a chest containing a Crystal Fragment, some Rusted Scrap nearby, and a group of chickens you can slice up for 3 Poultry (and you may as well give them to The Duke now to gain more points to the next meal).

Heading over to the inactive windmill, check the left side for some Handgun Ammo, and then check near the barrel for a small platform with the crank - which predictably breaks off in your hands. The earlier note mentioned one of the other windmills had a better crank, so that's your next objective.

Goat of Warding - Be sure to look around at the other side of the windmill to find a Goat of Warding that's hiding among a pile of logs.

Head inside and go down the windmill to come out onto the flooded fishing village. There's a path among the crumbling rooftops and debris here, and note that small floating platform that causes you to move slowly across it.

At the end of the roof, look for another platform with yellow tape you can attack to cause the platform to drop down as a bridge. However, as you approach, Moreau will crash into the floating platforms. Be sure to hold off for a moment, as he'll double back quickly to crash into it again, and once he starts to swim in a large circle off to the right, dash across the platform.

On the next roof, there's two floating platforms - one longer than the other. Wait again for him to start swimming away before you cross the right platform that leads to a tall section of wood you can slice - but there's a support on the other side that needs to be cut.

Carefully go back and wait until Moreau crashes through on the way to the other side.

Step onto the long floating platform, and you may hear Moreau call out as he moves towards you. Hop back and wait until he crashes by to quickly dash out to the end of the floating platform, aim up to the right and shoot down the last yellow tape to create a new bridge.

Move back to the right and continue on. Thankfully Moreau is pretty nice about not trying to kill you unless you're on shaky floating platforms, so move into the shack and head out the back to find a barrel to break

Climb up the short stairs and push the minecart into the water - but it looks like you need another platform to cross.

Hop down and you'll find a nearby switch to raise up a new minecart - but you'll need to take a long detour to get back there.

Goat of Warding - it may be hard to spot, but look out across the water from the building with the minecarts towards the broken windmill in the distance to spot some large wooden beams sticking vertically out of the water like a ship's mast. At the top of these planks is lone bobbling goat perched precariously, and you'll need to snipe it from a distance.

Crossing over to the next walkway, you'll see several sunken platforms with different colored tape. The corresponding switches will briefly raise these platforms, but not for too long so you'll want to be quick.

Start by pressing the blue lever and hurrying right to hit the red lever, allowing you to quickly hit the second blue lever before the next blue platform goes down, and sprint over to the shack before both platforms resubmerge.

Take note of the red and blue levers here, and then move to the back and break a crate next to a white lever. Since it corresponds to the furthest platform back on the boardwalk you came from, you'll want to hit the red and blue levers first, then hit the white lever before dashing across as fast as possible back the way you came, then right across all three colored platforms.

Cautiously make your way across the next floating platform, and wait when you get to the longer floating platform, as Moreau will crash through it once, then appear right in front of you, before finally swimming away.

When he shouts out as you cross the next long floating platform, quickly move to the left to catch a breather next to a barrel you can break. Take a careful step back onto the floating platforms to get him to charge again, then sprint past after his initial pass.

Finally, push a minecart forward to create a path back to the shack with the other minecart you raised, and push that one down to make a bridge to the next building and run across. Break the nearby barrel, and then cut down the wall of green goo to pass through the house.

Go up the ladder on the far side, and hit the lever to dredge up the shipwreck you can use to cross down to the windmill.

Move fast, because unlike the other parts of the fishing village, Moreau will have no qualms about trying to ram and destroy the ship. He'll summon a wall of green goo to try and stop you, so you may want to opt for the pistol instead of the knife to destroy it quickly before he tears down the ship.

Moving into the dark windmill base, move around to the far side to reach a dead end, and follow the yellow line to look up for a ladder locked by a padlock, and smash it with your knife so you can climb up top.

Once outside, Moreau will try and rattle you by ramming the place, but you're not really in any danger.

Break a nearby barrel, and look for the Crank on this mill's platform. As you move to the far side of the mill, you'll find there's part of a ladder going up, but it's been destroyed.

If you go back and use the Crank where you found it, you can reposition the mill so that a new ladder is formed, letting you climb to the very top.

From here, you can utilize your Crank to make a zipline back to the first mill, and then use it to power up the mill!

- Open the Sluice Gate

Head back down to the gatehouse, save and resupply if you need to, and then inspect the now powered gate controls.

For this puzzle, you need to match the colors on the panel to the picture displayed next to it, but a quick glance may tell you something's not quite right. There's a black square on the middle right, but the paper displays it differently. This is because the paper is on its side, so rotate it to make the black square on the same spot as the console. Now you'll be able to correctly color code the console:

With the console correctly coded, pull the nearby lever, and the reservoir will drain completely, stranding Moreau and opening up the way out of this hell.

Leave out the lower door to the right of the gate controls to survey the drained fishing village, and you'll spot Moreau trying to run away to the right of the mill.

Follow him and break a barrel on the left before entering a small shack. Inside in a drawer on the right you can find Moreau's Diary 1 File, and on the left is a small case with an M1911 - High-Capacity Mag that you should equip right now.

Boss Fight - Salvatore Moreau

He may be a fish out of water, but make no mistake, this version of Moreau is not to be taken lightly. Much like Lady Dimitrescu, Moreau's mutation will leave a humanoid portion of him guarded inside the mouth of a larger beast - and only the human portion is vulnerable to attack.

Unfortunately, the humanoid part of him doesn't reveal itself all too often, mostly after one of his attacks, which usually come in the form of him projectile vomiting acid at great distances. You'll need to either hit him with a stunning blast from a strong weapon to interrupt him, or duck around a corner when this happens, then dart back in and unload on him. He can also start to dive at you at a very fast speed and try to ram you, in which case you'll want to duck into one of the safe spots in this arena.

There are four such "safety spots" in this arena - one where you started that has a barrel along with Rusted Scrap and Chem Fluid. Two in the middle row that has another barrel with Shotgun Ammo and Rusted Scrap, the other with two Mines, Shotgun Ammo, Metal Scrap, and Gunpowder. Finally, one on the far side with a barrel alongside Handgun Ammo, First Aid Med, and another Mine.

Speaking of mines, one of the best ways to get Moreau stunned is to lay an ambush down. Luckily you have the mines, plus there are three explosive barrels - one by the top middle safe spot, one by the back row, and one by a small path between buildings Moreau will crash through at some point in the battle.

Using these or mines you can stun him with a large explosive attack, then follow up on his exposed weak spot with explosive rounds from your launcher, or unload your shotgun into his face.

Be wary when he starts to climb to the roof and talks about one of his special moves. He'll start spewing acid into the sky to literally make it rain, and it will deal a ton of damage unless you get away. The safe spots with the loot you find also double as cover from the rain - so when in doubt, look for the yellow marking around each area to know where to take cover.

During this period he may create giant goo barriers, which can be very annoying to deal with when trying to backpedal away from him. Always be aware of your escape options, and fire off a few pistol rounds to quickly get rid of any walls.

Watch out when he inflates to a huge size when wandering around - as he'll start spewing large spouts of acid while chasing you, requiring you to move fast and duck around corners to stay out of his way - and on his hind legs he's usually too high up for most explosions to phase him.

Sometimes when he goes in for a lunging attack, he'll briefly show his face, giving you just a moment to unload a shotgun or explosive round to knock him out of the attack.

As long as you time your attacks well and use your automatic pistol to get off some quick shots while saving your bigger hits for when you know he's exposed, the disgusting fishman will fall before you, offering up a Crystal Moreau. Be sure to loot the rest of the area if you haven't already, then get ready to leave.

Head up the far path and break a barrel outside the mine entrance, and head inside to another barrel and then go left up to where you first spotted Moreau.

Inside you can find Moreau's Diary 2 File, a Cadou specimen that seems to be at the root of these infected people, and the next upgrade for your key, making it the Six-Winged Unborn Key.

You'll be interrupted by the fourth and final lord, Karl Heisenberg, who offers an interesting and dubious proposal. Your next stop seems to be a stronghold near the Village, but there's a few more things to do here first.

Important - Once you take the lift out of the mines, it won't work again, so be sure you've gotten everything from the mines, and checked out what's changed since the water level has gone down - which is highlighted below!

With that in mind, head back through the mines to the boathouse, to find a path created by the draining water, heading down under the mill. There's even a barrel here you can break.

Goat of Warding - As you exit the other side of the mill, look to the left for a Goat of Warding perched right on some rocks.

Further down you'll find the remaining pool of water - all that's left of the reservoir, and two catfish that can be gutted for 4 Fish Meat. Plus, you can find the boat with the chest you may have spotted earlier, and finally open it to get a Silver Angel Statue.

Moreau's Lab

After you've taken the lift back up the first mill with the Labyrinth puzzle, you'll find that you can now open the mechanical gate on the right using the Crank.

Going up the mountain path, you'll find a fork - and it's best you go up the upper right path first to find a crate, and a bridge over to a small shrine that holds the Mermaid Ball needed for the Labyrinth back down below.

Turning around, you can spot two winged Samcas flying around the two nearby buildings, with a third perched on a high hill nearby. Be sure to snipe one or two of them and then sneak up on the one perched at the top and grab the Herb next to the zipline.

Cautiously advance into the two large buildings between the giant pile of dead beasts, and you'll find a few Moroaicas inside to kill, along with a crate and Sniper Rifle Ammo in one building, and a bunch of Handgun Ammo in the other.

Before going to the last house, check the path past the last house to come down to a crate and a well that you can use the Well Wheel to get some Flashbangs, you'll likely want to use them soon enough.

As you head up to the third building on the small hill, you can probably hear the sounds of something inside. Slowly move around the left of the building to find some Shotgun Ammo by a pile of wood. Move around to the back of the building to find a small hole to crawl through, allowing you to get the drop on the Lycan by the door and blow off his head.

Read Moreau's Diary of Experiments File on the desk, and then open the nearby chest to find the coveted M1851 Wolfsbane Revolver a true powerhouse of a weapon. You may have already found a few Magnum Rounds already, which is good - because something has decided to come up the hill to find you.

Another Varcolac werewolf is now stalking the giant bloody pile down the hill, and it will make great target practice for your new weapon.

In order to make every shot count, it's highly recommended you make use of the Grenade Launcher's Flashbang rounds to stun the giant beast after sniping it from a distance to weaken it, and then let loose a few magnum shots to the face to finish it off quickly.

If things get dicey and you need some space, remember you can use the zipline up the hill to get some distance on the creature, or hide in the houses.

Finally, you can now return to the Labyrinth by the windmill and use the Mermaid Ball to activate the puzzle. It's a fairly straightforward one, as you need only follow the rails and carefully move onto the water wheel to drop down to the next level.

After dropping down again, hug the right wall to avoid an open ledge on the left, and then wrap around down to the bottom to complete the puzzle, earning you a Chartreuse Skull worth a ton of money.

The Village (Fourth Visit)

Heading Back to the Village

While there's not much that has changed in the village beyond Heisenberg's flair for the dramatic directing you towards the Stronghold, there are a few new things you can make use of with your new Crank.

First things first, be sure to move to the back left corner of East Old Town to finally open the mechanical door using the Crank, and help yourself to the defenseless chickens here for 2 Poultry.

There's also an outhouse here, but it's already open, and there's an arrow pointing to the left. Back up a bit and look under the house on the left to spot an open jar, and look inside to get Yellow Quartz.

There's also a nearby ladder that will take you up to a small ledge overlooking East Old Town. Carefully move along the ledge, and you can drop down onto the roof of a shed near a dead body, and open the chest near the body to claim a Pigeon Blood Ruby.

Before heading back to the Altar, follow Heisenberg's signs to the Graveyard, where two black mountain goats have taken up residence. Slice them up (and watch they don't kick you) for 4 Meat, then return to The Duke to hand in your food.

The River Boat Treasures

From the Altar, start making your way back to the Ceremony Site, but stop at the large bridge. If you go down to the right, you can lower the drawbridge on the side using your new Crank.

Cross the drawbridge and you'll find a crate and a boat you can use to ride up and down the river.

Start by taking the boat north towards Castle Dimitrescu. While you can't re-enter the castle here, you can disembark at a small dock and lower a crank back to the Craftsman's Hut outside the Tower of Worship.

Be sure to head into the back of the shack and open the outhouse for Gunpowder if you missed it last time, and to use the Well Wheel to dredge up the well and find... a ladder down?

Descend into the well and look in the puddles of water to find a Lockpick, and then move forward to find a room full of hanging spike traps. They won't fall on you, but there's a puzzle to solve if you want to get what's behind the locked gate at the far end.

Start by grabbing a Mine on the right, then move towards the locked gate, and climb up onto the raised platform on the right, and up to another raised platform to reach a ledge. There's a Pipe Bomb here, but more importantly is a control panel that raises and lowers a few of the spike traps.

Hit the two white lights to bring up both platforms at the far end up - including the one with the minecart on it.

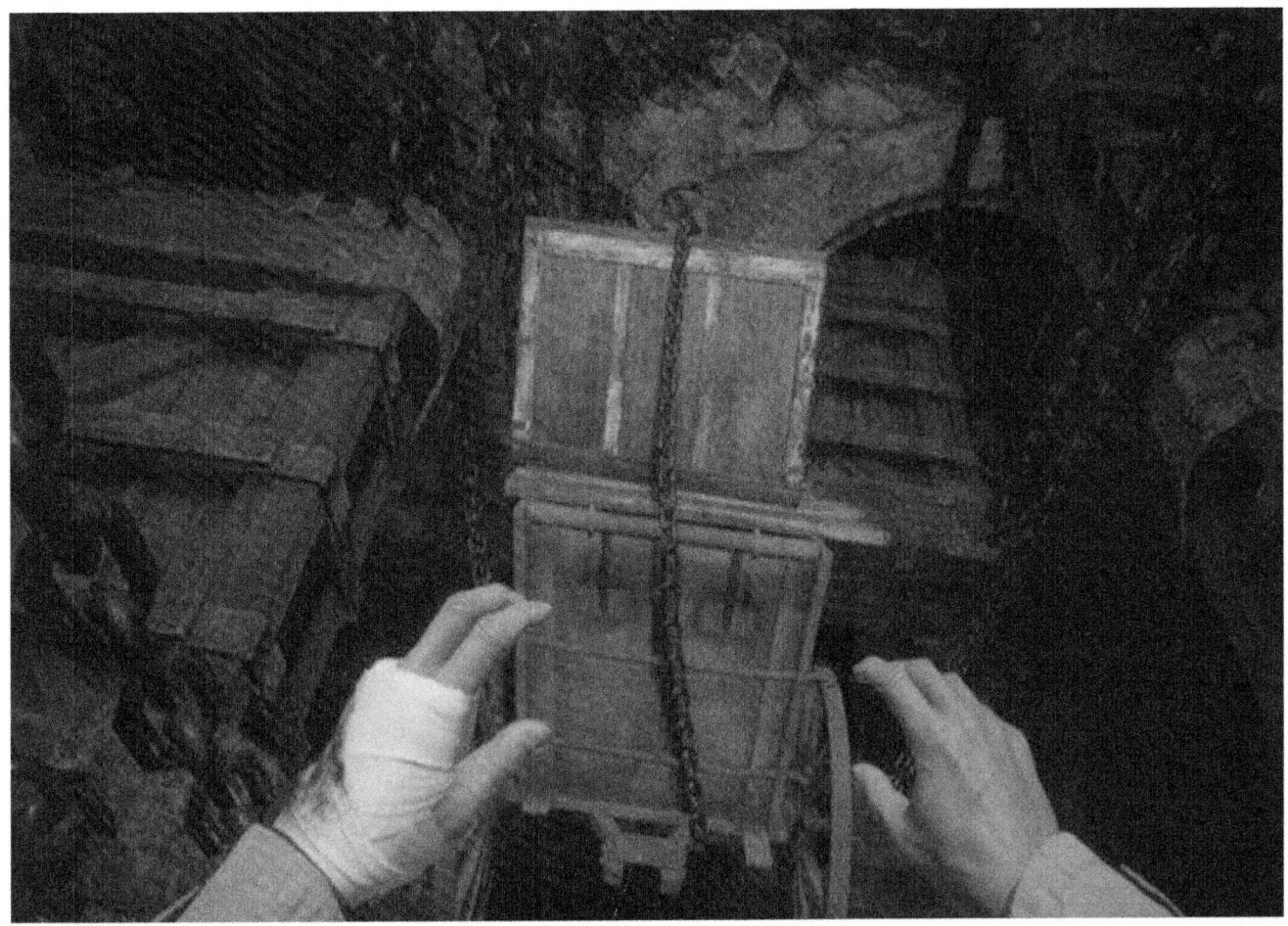

Cross to the other side and grab some Shotgun Ammo along the rocks, and then push the nearby cart forward until you can reach the minecart on the platform, and then push it off down below. This will create a platform to get you over to the ledge with the crate you can break.

Now, drop down into the hole, and open the chest for a Large Pigeon Blood Ruby, and look under the torture rack for Flashbangs and Magnum Ammo. Unlocking the door will pull up all the spike trap platforms - but don't worry, they won't be coming down again.

You should now have both Pigeon Blood Rubies - which you can combine with the Necklace with two holes to complete the treasure - Dimitrescu's Necklace!

Back across the drawbridge, look for a door with torches on the side to enter a treasure hold.

This secret area features two unlit torches with a swinging brazier in the middle, and a second unlit torch in the far room, along with a crate.

To unlock the three doors, start by lighting the two torches in the first room. While you can try your luck at pushing, it's much easier to crouch down behind the brazier to angle your pistol shot upward so the brazier swings hard into the torch - then do the same for the other side.

The doors will unlock as the torches are lit - the one on the left holds a treasure trove of Lei, while the other door has a few crates, and a hole in the wall that a Ghoul will start crawling out of. At this point you'll notice two things:

The second room with the torch can't be reached by the swinging brazier, and killing the ghoul will only make a new one crawl out.

Putting two and two together, you'll need to use the Ghoul as a flammable guinea pig. Let him stumble after you into the brazier room and push it into his face, lighting the poor guy on fire.

This won't kill him outright, so you can have the burning zombie chase you into the next room, and make him lunge at the torch to open the final room - then kill him.

Inside you'll find the grand treasure - the Golden Lady Statue, which is worth a decent amount of money when sold to The Duke. Be sure to also check the table for Magnum Ammo, then head back to the boat.

Taking the riverboat south away from the Castle and down towards the Reservoir, you'll reach a dead end with a dock to disembark at. Take the left path first to find a small fishing hole with a rare fish, netting you the Finest Fish Meat, along with 2 more Fish Meat if you missed some earlier.

Take the right path next, and enter a small tunnel that opens into a large cavern with giant roots in an even bigger pit. As you move forward, something loud in the depths of this cavern will sound out - but keep moving forward to find a small campsite.

There's a ton of free loot here, including Handgun Ammo, an Antique Coin straight out of Resident Evil 7, 2 Mines, as well as Flashbangs and Explosive Rounds. A nearby metal case can be opened to obtain the W870 TAC - Foregrip Mod for the shotgun.

Finally, check the computer for the Analysis Results File, which mentions that the fungal colony found under this village appears to be the source of the "mold" infection that was let loose at the Baker compound in the previous game.

If you needed any more evidence, the roots will begin writhing as you make your way back - not unlike how the Evelyn bioweapon looked at the end of RE7.

This will also trigger 3 Ghouls to climb onto the path, so be ready to deal with them quickly and then head back to the Village.

Otto's Mill

As you start to follow Heisenberg's trail of signs out of the village, you may want to consider taking a slight detour past the church to the Fallow Plot.

A roar will alert you that the large field is now home to a great and terrible beast - an even bigger and more ancient werewolf than those you fought previously.

This beast, like the others, can move fast and strike extremely hard, and will require a bit more firepower to take out, but can be evaded inside buildings.

This is also a great use of your grenade launcher's flashbangs - after starting the fight by sniping the creature's head a few times, prepare your flashbang as it charges, and then once it's stunned, follow up with a few magnum rounds, shotgun hits, or explosive rounds to the face.

You can also further set up your ambush by placing a mine a little ahead of you, timing its explosion with your flashbang, and then if the beast still stands, run into the shack on the left and use the flour bags (if they are still there) to further stun it as it tries to follow.

Deal enough damage, and the imposing beast will fall, and you'll gain its Crystal Ancient Beast which sells for a huge sum of Lei to The Duke.

Back on the path to the Stronghold, use the Six Wing Unborn Key, but take the left path at the last "Good Luck" sign to come out onto a large lumber mill. Ignore the explosive barrels in the river for now, and instead start exploring outside.

Goat of Warding - Under the mill itself, look for a small shrine in the middle of the stream to find another goat you can destroy.

Since the door on the right side of the mill is locked, cross the stream to the far side to find a crate near a padlocked gate you can destroy. Inside the pen is a pig you can gut for 2 Meat, and a trove of items including a crate and 2 Mines. Turn around from them and you can find a Crystal Fragment atop an old snow-covered generator, then head inside the mill.

A loud scream will ring out as you enter, followed by loud thudding noises. As you move into the main mill room, you'll find out why.

Another giant enemy with an equally giant axe - the same as the one from the garden graveyard - makes his home here, and he does not like intruders.

Unlike the other giant fight, you'll have a lot more room to maneuver here. This is good, because the giant will employ a lot of sweeping attack, especially when he holds his axe in a low sweeping stance or high overhead stance. He can and will also jump great distances to strike down on you, so you should constantly be on the move as you fight this enemy.

Use everything in your disposal to slow him down - plant mines, toss pipe bombs, and use explosive rounds when he's standing still, and make use of the ammo scattered around the mill.

At certain points he'll call out for backup, but there won't be ghouls this time. Instead, he'll summon Winged Creatures to help him fight. This is actually not as bad as it sounds, as these enemies usually dart around for a long time before attacking, and you can usually either catch them with an explosive blast from your weapons, or quickly turn and fill them with shotgun shells to kill them quickly. There are also two red barrels you can utilize both to interrupt the giant, and tear apart any friends he has at the same time.

Remember that the Winged Creatures will also drop even more crafting resources should you start to run low on ammo. He's pretty vulnerable when calling for help, so take that time to unload some sniper rifle shots on his face, or hit him point blank with a shotgun a few times before running away.

When the giant axe man finally falls, gather his Giant Crystal Axe and slice open all three padlocks on the far door. Make sure you've cleaned the place out for ammo and head into the next room.

In the cannibal's storehouse, you can find a ton of meat to give to the Duke, including 3 Meat, 1 Poultry, and 1 Fish Meat. The room also has an Herb to replenish your health, as well as Metal Scrap, and Ernest's Diary File on the table.

Finally, enter the last room to find a small table with a chest holding the real prize - Father Nichola's Angel. Grab the Gunpowder and bust the two crates on the far shelf before you leave, and then head outside.

Unfortunately, a group of Lycans will try to rush you from the exit to the mill, but lucky for you there happen to be several explosive barrels lining the stream. Try and lure a group of them near one and explode it to take them all out, then wait for any stragglers and repeat the process, and they'll all fall easily to your trap.

Now it's time to infiltrate that Stronghold, and hope Heisenberg doesn't have anything nasty in store for you.

The Stronghold

Path to the Stronghold

When you're ready to see what Heisenberg has in store for you, head through the tunnel stairs going up to the Stronghold.

Be ready for a lycan attack as you reach an open area with several ledges - and take the path up to a small bridge overlooking the area.

As you move toward the right, the Lycans will begin their attack, but you'll be next to a trough with some Rusted Scrap and bags of flour. Use it to stun the group of attackers as they advance on you so that they can be eliminated before they deal any damage.

Move towards the group of burning bodies to find an Herb, and look ahead to spot a few more Lycan waiting along the ridges - if they aren't moving yet, get off some sniper shots to clear the herd before you mop up the rest. There's also another Herb growing on the far left wall.

Take the left path and watch for more Lycans jumping down from above, and then advance cautiously to find two Lycan Archers trying to shoot you from the ruins. Use your sniper rifle if you can to fight back, then advance to the nearby cover with a breakable crate. There's another crate on the right before you enter the ruins yourself.

Note the explosive barrel as you enter the courtyard in the ruins, and grab a nearby Mine and break the crates around before heading up.

As you move around the platform above where you entered, another Lycan attack will begin, and if you look back down in the courtyard you can spot a few massing by the explosive barrel that will make a juicy target.

Run to the nearby archer next, and snipe the other one before clearing out any more advancing Lycans.

Entering the large area in front of the Stronghold gate, take note of the two explosive barrels on the right, and one on a high ledge to the left.

Break the nearby crates and grab the Handgun Ammo and Shotgun Ammo first before moving to the upper levels where there's two different levers to open the gate.

Head up the stairs to the lever to the left of the door - on the same side as the explosive barrel, and be sure to grab the Sniper Rifle Ammo first, and then pull the first lever.

A group of Lycans will run in, and you may want to trigger one of the explosive barrels as they rush through the center. Be sure to also place a mine or two on the stairs where they are forced to bunch up, and mow the rest down with your shotgun.

There's a chance one or two may hop across the raised platforms to get at you from your back, so be sure to pivot and check your sides to make sure you don't get ambushed.

When the wave dies down, place another mine, and be ready for a few more to show up on the raised platforms and start jumping towards you.

Snipe a few if you can while they roar, then defend your position at the top.

Once the second wave is gone, go down and loot the dead before climbing the ladder to the other lever. The gate is now opened, and you can enter the Stronghold.

Stronghold

Entering the large first chamber, use the Save Point, and grab the Pipe Bomb next to it, and some Rusted Scrap in an open barrel as you break the nearby crates.

You can also look up to the right along the broken stairwell to spot a shiny point to shoot, and grab a Yellow Quartz.

As you move into the large main stronghold room, be ready, because this room is going to have a lot of enemies in it. There's an explosive barrel below you, as well as one on the far side.

If you cross to the middle of the room, a Lycan horde will appear, and you can detonate the barrel - plus throw a pipe bomb at the short bridge as the group tries to cross over to you.

If you still have a large group chasing you, run across the bridge and hang right to find a stairway down to the bottom where you can run past the barrel and then turn to explode it as they follow.

Then, look for some barrels at the back for a First Aid Med and Pipe Bomb that will come in handy.

The Lycans will keep coming, so sprint back up the stairs and to the far left side onto some scaffolding where you can get to a zipline to cross to the far side. If there's a group bunched up chasing you, try shooting an explosive grenade to clear the area first.

Moving up the stairs to the top level, grab some Sniper Rifle Ammo as you cross to the far side, and be ready, because another horde led by an Armored Lycan is standing between you and the exit.

Try stunning them with a flashbang if possible, and follow up with a Pipebomb or two while they can't see you, and place a mine and back up once their vision clears. This will likely clear out a large group of them, and you'll be able to mop up the rest with your shotgun before pressing on.

The Lycans won't follow you into this next circular room, so you'll have a bit of a breather. Look near a suit of armor for Gunpowder and Magnum Ammo before heading down the staircase. Be on the lookout for Metal Scrap and a crate to break as you move down to the bottom.

Goat of Warding - Once you reach the bottom of the stairwell, look along the railing to the right to spot a bobbling Goat of Warding to smash before moving on.

As you move through the narrow passage and watch the Lycans feed, you'll come out into a small cave. Grab some First Aid Med on the right, Explosive Rounds and Sniper Rifle Ammo on the left, and look for an Officer's Diary File on the ground before using the nearby Save Point.

Mini-Boss Fight - Urias

The big wild-maned Lycan boss with the hammer you first met in the Village is back with a vengeance, and this time you need to put him down.

If you faced the Giants elsewhere in the Village, the fight will play similarly. He can leap at you from the upper ledge, so quickly run under his jump, turn, and fire an explosive round to knock him back, and follow up with shotgun blasts.

When he rears back his hammer, get some distance and use the rocky walls and pillars to make sure he can't hit you with his spinning sweep attack. When his hammer knocks back against the walls, use that time to get some shots off.

He may also put away his hammer and walk towards a pillar. If he does this, quickly run past him and hide behind another pillar so you can't get hit when he throws it.

If he jumps back to the platform above and roar for backup, bringing more Lycans into the fight. Hold off on launching a Pipe Bomb or Explosive Round until they jump down around him, and then let loose to destroy the smaller enemies.

If you run low on ammo, check the small alcoves on the side to find plenty of Pipe Bombs, a First Aid Med, and Ammo for all your weapons.

Keep moving and never let yourself get cornered, ducking past him after one of his assaults, and use the rocky outcroppings for covers when you run out of pillars to hide behind.

If you have any magnum rounds, make sure you have a clear shot after one of his attacks to strike his head, and let loose a few, and he should go down before long, leaving the Crystal Hammer behind to loot for some serious cash.

In the chamber beyond is a large crystal formation full of jewels. Inspect the place carefully and shoot down any glowing spots to get 1 Large Crystal, 4 Crystal Fragment, 1 Vivianite, and 1 Yellow Quartz.

There's a few crates to break in the chamber below where you'll also find the last piece of the puzzle, the Torso Flask. Heisenberg has another message for you - and wants you to put all the flasks you have assembled into the main Altar back at the village.

Heading out of here is easy - just pass through the next hall, and be sure to grab Guglielmo's Plate on the left before taking the small boat up the underground stream to dock not far away - with a ladder heading topside to the cemetery behind the church.

Before you leave, there's a small passage to the left you can take to a prison/lab of some sort.

There's a few crates to break and Chem Fluid in one of the cells next to a Photo of a Phantom Fish, pointing out the golden fish you may have already killed down the river from the Lone Road.

Against the far chamber at the end you can spot a Pipe Bomb and Shotgun Ammo, as well as an Experiment Notes File detailing how the Cadou parasite has affected various hosts - one of whose names may be familiar to you.

Be wary on your way out, as several Moroaica ghouls will crawl out to ambush you - but they are nothing a well placed Pipe Bomb or Mine can't take care of.

Heisenberg's Factory

Reach Heisenberg's Factory

- Complete the Chalice

By now, you will have all four of Rose's Flasks, the Head, Torso, Arms, and Legs. Return to the Altar, sell all your treasure and buy any upgrades you need from The Duke, and save your progress.

Approach the Altar and place all four Flasks into the receptacle, which will come unlocked to give you the Giant's Chalice. With this new object in your possession, you can now approach the large dias at the Ceremony Site where the four giant statues of each house are located.

Important - Make sure you have everything you need before proceeding forward. You won't be able to do any more re-exploring and backtracking once you enter the Factory, so this is the last time you'll be able to hunt wild animals or track down missing treasure!

- Find Heisenberg

Once you place the chalice on the dias, a scene will occur that will raise a giant bridge over to Heisenberg's Factory, clearing the way for your next confrontation. You'll be taken down to a lower level as you cross over to his factory, and told to go inside to meet him.

The Factory

There's not much to note in the large field leading up to his factory entrance, other than some Rusted Scrap and Metal Scrap in the back of some wrecked cars on either side.

The old barn-like entrance is eerily quiet, and a larger gate inside is locked, forcing you to head left to grab some Gunpowder off the shelves and find a door going deeper underground.

Follow the path into another large room to grab some Chem Fluid off the table, then turn right and inspect a large wall covered by cloth.

You'll get a moment to see Heisenberg's grand spider-tape plan before the man himself appears to fill you in on his grand plan. Ethan won't exactly agree to this shaky team up, and so you'll be unceremoniously cast into the factory to meet Heisernberg's little pet.

As soon as you get up, you'll need to hurry away from the man with the propeller blade stuck on his face. Nothing you do will hurt it right now, so run, and turn right as the door ahead closes to duck through a hole in the wall, and then continue right.

The monster behind you won't care much for the door and break it open, forcing you to keep running as you duck under some debris. When you hit another dead end, look to the right for a chute to take you far down into the depths of Heisenberg's Factory.

The Factory B4 - Materials

You'll come out into a giant scrap pile, but at least the monster isn't following you anymore. Make your way through the pile and look for assorted Rusted Scrap, Gunpowder, and Metal Scrap as you climb up to the left. Look for a ladder along the wall you can hop up to.

It won't be long before you run into more of Hiesenberg's creations - these are much like the ghouls you've fought previously, but the armor on their head must be knocked off first with a shot before you can get some actual headshots in. Since they tend to bunch up, you can also lay waste to them with an explosion of your choice to clear the road, and then move to the far side to pick up some Rusted Scrap, and look left for a wall grate you can open.

Take the next ladder up to find yourself in the heart of the factory, where Heisenberg has been busy building an army of his own. There's a crate behind you to break, and as you move to the right, you'll find The Duke has already set up shop on the lift you can open to one side.

Save here if you need to, and note that The Duke now has two new weapon variants for purchase, the V61 Custom Handgun, and SYG-12 Shotgun. An automatic machine pistol and semi-automatic focus firing shotgun, these are both great weapons that cost a small fortune to obtain - and unless you're willing to sell your old pistols and shotguns, you may need to buy his last inventory expansion too. The choice is yours if you'd rather keep upgrading your current weapons or invest in one or both of the new ones - as well as investing in the mods you can buy for each of them.

Since you can't use the lift he's in right now, exit and note the overall map of the factory floors, and check the door to the right to find a room with the final Labyrinth puzzle, as well as Rusted Scrap and Chem Fluid

Leave the room behind and enter the main doors to the right to find some long hallways to traverse leading to a room with a red-light door.

Grab some Gunpowder to the right first, then slash the red light with your knife. Be ready to take out two enemies on the other side of the door, so use those long hallways to give yourself room to mow them down.

The next room is dark, and there seems to be a gap in the platform leading to a far door, but the generator is offline.

Head down to the bottom level and be ready for two more enemies to burst out of the far door. Look for a crate you can break on the left and right of the door before moving inside.

Inside the Foundry, there's a large Casting Machine against the far wall that will be central to solving a few puzzles in the Factory. Look to the right for some x-ray photos of Heisenberg's experiments as well as some Chem Fluid, as well as some Rusted Scrap on a nearby table.

You can't interact with a strange hole in the wall, and another door is locked, leaving only one way out of the room for now. Going up the hall, three more ghouls are stumbling around a walkway, and can be bunched up nicely for an explosion to send them flying.

Note the cabinet on the left you can use a Lockpick on to gain a Yellow Quartz. Grab the Gunpowder on a barrel up ahead, and note the unpowered switch for a door, forcing you towards a far door into a lab area.

Besides some Rusted Scrap to the left, there's a creepy body with a drill for an arm in the next room, and if you think it's going to jump out and grab you - you might be right!

Move past the body for now into the next room and open a chest that has a Relief Mold you can use back in the Foundry.

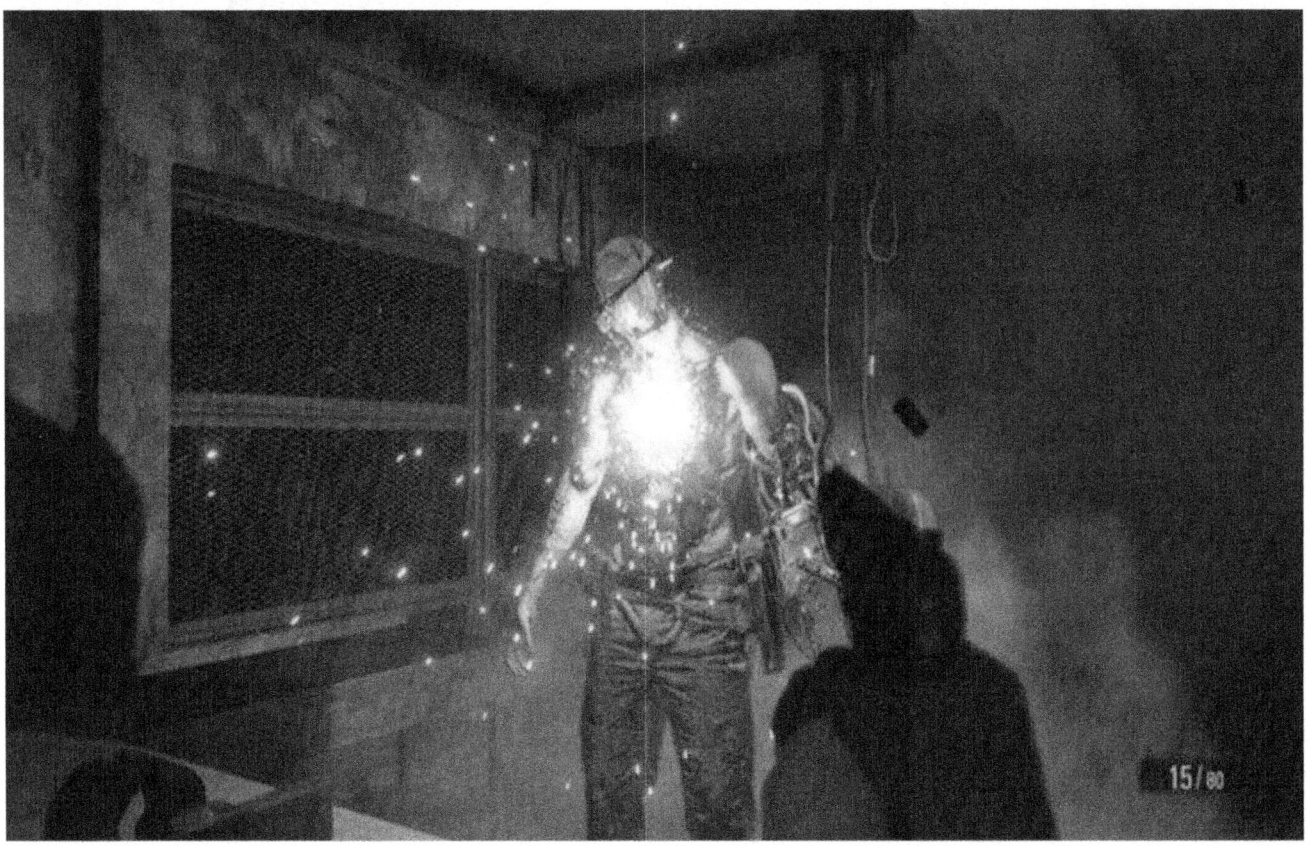

As expected, the enemy known as the Soldat will power up off his chair and move to attack. These enemies are extremely sturdy and can block shots with their drill arm, and deal some major damage if you get hit. Luckily, they move fairly slow, and take a few moments to swing or stab with their main weapon - which also leaves the large red light on their chest vulnerable to attack.

Get some distance on them using the nearby hallways and goad them into attacking then sprint away, pivot, and ready your rifle to zero in on their weak points. Dealing enough damage will short circuit them out, killing them instantly, and rewarding you with a Crystal Mechanical Heart.

Back in the Foundry, use the Relief Mold to obtain a Relief of a Horse, which you can then place on the hole in the wall behind you. This passage leads up to another ghoul, and a locked door to Heisenberg's Quarters that can't be accessed yet.

Turn around and inspect the desk to use a Lockpick and get some Magnum Ammo, and then move to drop down into the large Engine Room downstairs. Hit the crate behind you, and then look at the large engine machines that dot the zig-zagging walkway through this room.

The giant pistons here will move back and forth rapidly, swinging in front of the narrow parts of each walkway - and can damage you relentlessly if you move slowly beneath them. If you are worried sprinting won't be enough, you can shoot the red dots on each piston to stop them and give you safe passage - but you'll still have to worry about the ghouls up ahead.

You can actually take a few potshots at the enemies on the far side with your pistol, which will cause them to slowly stumble around to find you, and most likely get them killed trying to get past the large damaging pistons. Three more will appear in the middle section once you cross, so you'll either have to quickly sprint back, or fight them head on without the help of the pistons.

When all enemies are dead, you can blow out the remaining pistons to travel safely across, and look where the enemies crawled in the middle of the room to find a crate and some Explosive Rounds.

Look for the final piston's red light on the wall behind it and carefully snipe it to access a ladder taking you back upstairs to find some Rusted Scrap near another wall grate.

The door next to you is locked, so instead you'll have to move down the hall full of Soldats just waiting to come alive - but they won't…. Yet. Head through and unlock the door back to the Foundry before moving further down the stairs in the previous room.

There's a cracked wall here, but you can leave it for now as you explore the rest of the room to find a breakable crate and a backup generator missing a gear.

Downstairs are a number of fences and a cabinet in the back with a Mine, as well as some Gunpowder nearby next to a fence. Going up the stairs to the right, you'll find a door with red lights you can smash to enter.

In this storeroom, check on the left for a Development Note 1 File on a table, and a

Factory Map (Lower Levels) to the right by some Gunpowder. Open the large case by the file to get the Cog Mold, and unlock the far door to get back into the hall full of Soldats.

Surprise! The Soldat at the very end will awaken and try to ambush you, so move back down the hall and take aim with your rifle at his mechanical heart. You can lead him on a merry chase back through the generator room, and he'll even cut down a few fences for you.

You may also be able to get him to smash the crumbling wall - but it's better to just leave a Mine in front of it and have him step on it, blowing the wall open and damaging the Soldat in the process.

With the wall completely broken, look inside to get some Shotgun Ammo and open a case with a Mechanical Part (Cylinder) treasure that can be combined with something later for a better sell value.

Move back into the Foundry to put the Cog Mold into the press and get yourself a Large Cog to insert into the backup generator. The production line will start up again, but not before another Soldat drops down off the moving belts above, and the gate behind you seals up.

You'll be in a lot closer quarters with this foe, so let him tear down the small gates to expose his weakpoint, and strafe around bigger obstacles to keep your distance until you can plant enough shots in his chest to finish him.

Move through the newly opened gate at the bottom and smash the crate before going left, and up ahead you can spot another Soldat patrolling off to the right. Go left first to get some more ammo in a crate, then cautiously follow him into the next room.

There are several narrow halls here where the Soldat patrols, but of special note is some red arcing electric fuse box in the middle.

If you wait until the Soldat gets close to it, you can shoot it to explode the box and stun the Soldat, letting you unload a few free shots before running away.

Be sure to look for some crates to break and a cabinet with Gunpowder as you evade the enemy here, then move through the far door on this level to find another crate and a cabinet with Sniper Rifle Ammo, and a Large Crystal you can shoot down from the yellow PA system near the door.

Back in the previous room, head upstairs to find another Soldat heading your way, and lure him back to the fuse box downstairs to stun and eliminate him - just be wary of his stumbling strikes that end with a fast forward lunge with his drill. Check back where he came out of to find some Explosive Rounds, then break the red lights on the door to the right to move onward.

Another long room with narrow corridors awaits you here, and as expected, it's far from safe. Head down the left path first to spot 3 Ghouls coming your way and toss an explosive device to cripple them. Check further down the left path and you'll get a breakable crate and a Mine in a cabinet for your trouble.

Moving to the opposite side of the room, there's a small alcove by the stairs with a dead Soldat in a bed behind a small gate. Remember this as you move up the stairs, as a giant shipping container will soon fall, revealing an even tougher variant of the Soldat.

This guy has TWO drill arms, and no weak point on his chest - it's on his back instead, making it harder to get off clear shots. Let him chase you back down the stairs and into the alcove, and he'll destroy the gate for you.

With that out of the way, lead him back to the middle of the room to find another fuse box you can shoot to stun him and unload on his back when you get the chance. When he starts swinging wildly, try to strafe around to get a shot at his side and hit when he turns his back, and your sniper rifle will make short work of him, earning you a Large Crystal Mechanical Heart.

Be sure to return to the alcove with the dead Soldat, as you'll find he was lying next to a table with thousands of Lei, and some Magnum Ammo to boot.

As you leave the alcove, look up the wall opposite the stairs to spot a glowing spot along the crack, and shoot it to get some Yellow Quartz. Finally, head through the container the Soldat dropped out of to find a cabinet with some Shotgun Ammo, and leave through the nearby door.

The Factory B3 - Manufacturing

You'll be back in the room with the missing platform, and now that you have the power on, you can hit the button to lower the platform into place.

Look against the wall above the far door by a pipe for another glowing spot to shoot and get another Yellow Quartz. At this point you can head right to return to The Duke to sell and save, or move forward.

The next hall has some Gunpowder to grab, and Shotgun Ammo in a nearby drawer. Move into the next room with three small corridors, and note the fuse box by the doorway as another improved Soldat heads your way.

Stun him with the fuse box, and then use the small corridors to quickly duck behind him and strike when he goes for his signature lunge attacks.

As soon as you move into the next room, ol' propeller face will try to ambush you again, so immediately dash right and duck under some debris to reach a large door to slam in his face. Luckily, it's strong enough that even after bashing it in, it will still hold and give you some safety. Before moving on, grab some Rusted Scrap, Metal Scrap, and Gunpowder.

You'll move out into a large open area overlooking the production line, and a nearby lift access means you can finally bring The Duke up to this level, and quickly get back down below. Since your goal is onward and upward, look for a ladder to the right and keep climbing.

Move across the broken ground and down to a drain pipe where you can break a crate before heading into a mining area. As Heisenberg talks about his plans, be ready to deal with some more Ghouls mining the ore in these narrow tunnels.

Take the small path on the right to find two such enemies, and then help yourself to a crate, 2 Pipe Bombs and an Herb.

Back on the main path, look up for a birdcage holding some loot you can shoot down, and move forward to find a large drill with three workers around it — so try and clump them together and let them walk on a mine or into a Pipe Bomb before mopping up survivors. Inside a nearby cabinet you'll find a Lockpick, and around the drill are some precious gems including a Large Crystal and Crystal Fragment.

Look for a small grate to crouch through, and at the other end, drop down into a long muddy hallway. Be sure to turn around first to spot another crumbing wall, and detonate it with an explosive to reach an area filled with gems, letting you obtain another 2 Large Crystals, Vivianite, and a Yellow Quartz.

Entering the Grinder Shaft, look up to spot large metal blades slicing tons of scrap down to size. The only way out is to go up, so start moving and grab some Gunpowder near the middle, and break the crate on the side by some Metal Scrap.

As you move up to the second level, two new enemies will rocket down towards you. A new variation of the Soldat, the Soldat Jet, they now have a jetpack and an even bigger helmet, making escape even harder now. They'll also crouch down to employ laser targeting, and then rocket forward to slam into you, and will slide along rails even if they don't hit you dead on to catch you at angles, so be sure to put a lot of distance when they crouch down.

Utilize Flashbangs to keep the duo stunned and disoriented while you follow up with precision shots, or lay mines down to stop their charging attacks. Don't let yourself get surrounded, and use explosives to stun them so you can try and move past to move to different levels, forcing them to fly around to find you and giving you more avenues of escape.

Once both of these enemies go down, keep traveling up breaking crates and looking for Rusted Scrap, and look up at the grinder to notice the large red lights surrounding the machine. Take out each one with a pistol, as well as the bright light in the exact middle, and the grinder will power down. You can now take the ladder up into the Grinder Shaft.

The Factory B2 - Electrical

Exiting the grinder, break the crate on the side before hurrying through the far door.

Head up the stairs and check the table on the right for Chem Fluid and the Development Note 2 File. Nearby is the Factory Map (Upper Levels) on a crate, and if you check your map, you should spy a hidden chamber near you.

Look up ahead near the stairs for a minecart, and move it out of the way to crawl through a duct into a secret room.

Here you'll find some Gunpowder and Handgun Ammo, but more importantly is a case that holds a Ball Mold, the device you need to access the last Labyrinth puzzle.

As you move close to the Ventilation hall, a large turbine will start pulling you in. Quickly aim and shoot at the red center to power it down and save yourself a painful death. Be sure to look back at the ledge you were pulled off for a tiny glowing point on the walkway you can shoot to get a Yellow Quartz.

Goat of Warding - While in the Ventilation area, head to the very edge overlooking the Grinder Shaft where some bulldozer blades keep the scrap back, and wedged in them you can find a little lost bobbling goat to destroy next to some Metal Scrap and Rusted Scrap..

Carefully make your way along the outer pipe at the end of the Ventilation area to climb up a small ladder to a hole you can climb through. Grab some Chem Fluid in the next room, and take the nearby lift up to the next level.

The Factory B1 - Storage

Move down the hall as Heisenberg taunts you, and in the next room shoot down the birdcage to the right for loot, and look to the left for Shotgun Rounds in a cabinet, as well as Explosive Rounds and a Key Mold against the far wall.

In the next area you'll find yourself high over the production line - but this also means you can move across the platforms to reach the Lift and bring The Duke up to this level.

Before that however, be sure to break a nearby crate, then look for a far ledge to fall down to a lower platform, and crawl along the large pipe to find Shotgun Ammo and 2 Mines, as well as a zipline back to the other side of the room where there's some Yellow Quartz in the wall.

Before moving further into this floor, we'll need to do a bit of healthy backtracking. Raise the lift with The Duke, and sell your new treasures to buy any upgrades you need. Head back down to B4.

Goat of Warding - A tricky wooden goat to spot, take a look out the open lift door as you ride down with The Duke. In between B1 and B3, there's a goat perched along the red support girders going down. You'll either need to be quick to spot and shoot it, or you can try climbing the ladder outside the lift on B3 and looking back to spot it above and snipe it.

Head back towards the Foundry by going through the main doors only to find the lights have gone out. Spooky.

Once you reach the room outside the Foundry, a glow-in-the-dark Soldat will appear, swinging wildly that always ends with a lunge attack. Back up and wait out these strikes to hit him in the chest after his lunges, and use the long hallways behind you to get more room.

Another Soldat is waiting in similar fashion inside the Foundry and will burst out the door, so let him come to you before blinding him with a Flashbang and unloading on his reactor.

Once he's dead, head inside and use the Casting Machine to make both the Iron Horse Ball, and Heisenberg's Key.

With the boss man's key in hand, you may remember there were two doors we couldn't unlock on this level earlier - one was unpowered, the other needed his key.

Head left from the Casting Machine first to travel up to where the now powered switch door was, leading to the Operating Room.

There's a drawer in the first room with Sniper Rifle Ammo, and a host of dead Soldats in the room beyond. Look for a Lockpick on the left as you enter, and some Flashbangs further up on the left.

Luckily none of these Soldats will awaken - but one behind the far door will, and will smash through to attack you. Snipe it as it does, then follow up with a flashbang to unload even more shots to kill it quickly.

Grab the Handgun Ammo by the door it opened, and inside you'll find a Medical Log you can listen to while looting the large case nearby for the M1851 Wolfsbane - Long Barrel Mod.

Return to the Foundry and exit through the opposite end to return to the platform with Heisenberg's Quarters.

Four Ghouls are wandering around his room now, so be ready with a mine or bomb to stun them all before finishing them off. There's some Rusted Scrap on the left table and back, along with some Gunpowder, but the real prize is the chest in the middle that holds the Mechanical Part (Shaft). When combined with the other Mechanical Part, you can craft Heisenberg's Hammer, which sells for a huge amount of Lei.

As you start to head back to the lift through the darkened room outside the Foundry, something will be clanking towards you in the dark. This is the Soldat Panzer, which is completely armored from head to toe and provides no weak spots.

In order to make your own, utilize your Explosive Shots from your grenade launcher, or Pipe Bombs, or set a Mine to start popping off the enemy's armor. Check after your explosions stagger him to see if you can spot the glowing red spot on his armor, then blind him and go in for the kill.

You can also try and stun him to juke past the behemoth, as he won't follow too far - but there's another waiting in the halls beyond, and you don't want to get stabbed in the back. If you manage to kill them both, you'll get Perfect Crystal Mechanical Hearts from both enemies, making it well worth the effort.

Back at the lift, be sure to head into the side room to use the Iron Horse Ball to play the last Labyrinth game. To begin, slowly move the ball around the circle but don't fall off at the very end as you move to the right.

When you move to the lower level, tilt into the gear and keep the ball pressed against the sides so it doesn't fall out until it reaches the other side (it can be hard to see, so be sure to use the camera turn button).

As it circles around the back, carefully slow down before you reach the next drop, and wait for the little orange trolley below to move all the way right before dropping down. Then you need only pass through the trolley on the left and drop down one final time before reaching the goal, and collect the Bister Skull, which is worth a small fortune!

Important - This will be the last time you get to talk with The Duke in The Factory, so it's time to sell all your treasure and buy all the upgrades you need.

Head back up to B1 with Heisenberg's Key and head into the next hall. Heisenberg is ready for you to meet his little pet, but before you do move into the first room to stock up. Inside you'll find a helpful Prototype: Sturm File, as well as crates to break and Mine, First Aid Med, and Handgun Ammo to collect.

Mini-Boss Fight - Sturm

You've met old propeller head before, but now you have a strategy for actually defeating him. Before we get to that, it's important to note the layout of this room is all full of winding walls and passages - but Sturm will pretty much destroy almost all of them. Like the juggernaut he is, he'll charge forward and break down stone walls with ease, but this will actually give you a lot more room to avoid him, so feel free to send him hurtling toward anything he doesn't break.

Once you get enough room to properly sidestep Sturm, let him charge into a wall he can't break, then run around behind him and unload on his weak spot on the back. You'll usually get a chance to unload at least one or two shots, so make them count. Be sure he breaks all the walls around the two larger metal sections of this room, as you'll want that cover before long.

After dealing a bunch of damage to his exposed point, Sturm will ignite in flames. Rather than weakening him, it'll actually just make him more mad and stronger. He'll start revving up while on fire, and that's your cue to get behind the giant metal boxes to avoid his flame wave attack.

Once he lashes out with his fires, he'll begin to charge again, but this time he'll quickly adapt to charge 2-3 times before really stopping, so don't look back until you're sure he's bounced off enough obstacles. Then, he'll let loose another flame wave and repeat the process. Keep avoiding him during this phase until his flames sputter out, at which point he'll charge like normal.

The process can be long and grueling, but as long as you stay one step ahead of him, and you can pick your shots with care - and even use a few Magnum rounds to quickly deplete his health. Once he starts to flail wildly and spark, he'll finally shut off for good, leaving behind the Complex Mechanical Heart.

With Sturm dead, grab any ammo along the walls you may have missed, and head into the next room to open a cabinet with First Aid Med, as well as Heisenberg's Cigar on a far table next to Heisenberg's Diary File.

Goat of Warding - You might hear the telltale bobbling of a nearby goat at this point. If you look at your map, you'll spot a small room nearby, and look around there's a small open vent to the right of the diary you can crawl through to a room that holds Shotgun Ammo in a drawer, as well as a Herb, Chem Fluid, and Metal Scrap along with the goat on top of a barrel.

Heading out into the Cargo Bay, break the two crates down here before carefully crossing the narrow metal pole to a lift to take you up to the ground floor.

You'll be back in the barn area of the factory, but it looks like Heisenberg isn't quite content to let you leave. You'll get a glimpse of his true power as he tosses you back down into the Factory. All the way to the bottom. Great.

With nothing else to do, look for a nearby grate to enter a Scrapheap, and inside you'll finally meet up with your old pal Chris, who will finally tell you what's really going on with Mother Miranda. Putting differences aside, Chris is ready to let you help take the fight to these freaks, and has even built a little present for you.

After Chris moves on to finish his mission in the Factory, be sure to save at the Typewriter here, and check the computer for Chris's Computer File. Look around the Scrapheap for a crate and some First Aid Med, then when you're ready, board the Fun Machine and head into the lift to face Heisenberg.

Boss Battle - Karl Heisenberg

With your polymer/metal composite death machine, you'll be able to take the fight to Heisenberg without him being able to manipulate your craft.

As you take the lift up to the field outside the Factory, take a minute to get a feel for the controls - including your machine gun, cannon, and blocking move.

Heisenberg is far from a pushover in his final form, and the arena you'll be in gives you a bit of breathing room, but not much.

It's especially hard to turn or get away from Heisenberg in your machine - but you'll find that your cannon attack doubles as a getaway move, blasting you back by a great distance, so try using it to evade some of his moves.

For this fight, you'll need to focus your fire entirely on the glowing red spots in Heisenberg's metal form, destroying the weak points with a combination of sustained machine gun fire and cannon blasts, while also using the blasts to get away from him.

If you see your machine gun fire eliciting red sparks on his body, you'll know you're hitting the right spot.

Heisenberg will alternate lifting one of his buzz saws before charging at you, and if you can't blast back, you'll need to hold your ground and block at the last possible second. Missing the timed block is bad news for this fight, as you won't be able to heal while in your machine. Instead, spend the fight doing a wide circle strafe around the arena, and make sure you have room behind you to blast backwards when needed.

At certain points, Heisenberg will summon giant metal plates to hide behind, but you can strafe around to find openings to keep up your fire. Blowing up one of his weak points will also stun him, which you can use to interrupt his charge attacks. He may also plant both saws down and charge forth - which is an ideal time to blast him with a cannon to stun his advance.

After dealing enough damage to his weak spots (destroying them all will just summon a new batch), he'll light on fire, and soon you'll be lifted into the air - and you can retaliate with a cannon blast to his face... but now you'll be on the ground with no machine to ride.

Since you can't hope to block his attacks in on foot, you'll need to run and gun by letting lose your explosive blasts and rifle fire at his head, then turning to get behind any debris to keep Heisenberg off you, and pivot only to let out a few shots before running away again.

He tends to charge in a straight line, so as long as you run diagonally, he'll have a hard time catching you with one of his swings, and move behind the large plates to keep a buffer between you.

Keep up the fire on his head, using your high powered shots to interrupt his attacks until he starts to generate a giant electrical field.

You'll be tossed into the sky again, but fate has one last cannon blast in store for Heisenberg, and the fight will conclude.

Unfortunately, things are going to take a very bad turn for Ethan following this battle. Still, the Finale must go on.

Finale

Assault on The Village

It's time for a change of perspective. You won't have access to the map anymore in this sequence, but what you do have is an impressive loadout. A semi-automatic USM-AI Pistol, and a fully automatic Dragoon Rifle that will tear through enemies, and plenty of ammo to spend - along with several grenades and a laser targeting device. It's time for some payback.

- Kill Miranda, Save Rose

Move through the woods with your squad until you reach the edge of the village, overlooking the ruins of Luiza's House. Check out the battle raging below before heading down yourself, and get ready to fight.

A few groups of Lycans will advance on you, but your weapons should make short work of them - don't worry about the ammo count, you'll be fine.

Once you reach Luiza's House, look for a crate with green smoke to restock on ammo and grab a few Flash Grenades as well.

As you move into the burning field, huge writhing roots of the Megamycete will burst out everywhere.

Further up, not one, but two Varcolac Werewolves will bound into view. Quickly hit them with a flash grenade and unload on one, then follow up with a regular grenade to send them flying, and quickly mop up the last one with a full clip. If you need to, there's still space around the field to run and gun if you have to.

Moving forward past the field, take a left through a newly opened road back to the first house Ethan explored. If you look to the left over where the Workshop is, there's another green smoke crate with a restock for you.

Take the left path through the house's small kennel, and you'll find that you also have auto-night vision goggles! Use them to take out the crew of Lycans, and move out onto the road on the other side.

A lot of waves of Lycans will start appearing on the road, including two archers, so use short bursts from your Dragoon to pick them off at a distance, then swap to your pistol when they get close before reloading both. Pick off the enemies on the roof, and don't worry about taking things slow, you don't want to get careless and overwhelmed this early.

Once the waves seem to die down, advance slowly and check a ruined house on the right for another green smoke restock crate. Some more Lycans will try to ambush you as you leave, so mow them down and snipe the archer on top before moving forward.

When you reach the tractor an Armored Lycan will appear with a large group - which is a good time to use one of those grenades to send them all flying. More waves will appear, so don't be afraid to slowly backpedal down the road to cut them down until they stop coming.

- Destroy the Mold Construct

When you at least reach the Village square, you'll finally get to start using your laser targeting device to punch some major holes in the Megamycete at the graveyard. You'll need to hold onto the targeting until it's fully complete and not break line of sight - plus it has a lengthy reload time.

Unfortunately, while you wait for the reload, groups of Lycans will come down to attack. Use your grenade to demolish them as they all jump down at once, and retreat back into the large nearby house. When prompted back away from the Lycans and use your laser targeting again, and the resulting bombardment will kill all Lycans in the area.

There's still another wave to go, so use the restock area by the large house and keep chucking more grenades to deal with clumps of Lycans and their Armored variants. You can also move through and around to the back of the house if you need to put some distance on the Lycans, and be sure to utilize the flash grenades to stun the group - giving you time to unleash another bombardment strike.

Finally, when the aerial strikes punch a hole in the writhing mass, you'll be able to head down underground. Grab some more supplies as you head inside, but be wary - something else is waiting for you down here.

The giant wolfman called Urias is down here, and this armored and twisted version is almost impervious to your attacks.

In such a small fighting arena, you'll need to constantly be moving and strafing to avoid his strikes, and wait for your laser targeting device to work again.

The good news is that he is vulnerable to attacks - but only on his back, so you can try to unload on him after jump strikes, toss any remaining grenades and flash grenades to stun him, and wait for those aerial strikes to finish the job. You'll get a Giant Crystal Mace for your trouble, and now it's time to move forward.

Once you reach the Megamycete chamber, you'll place some explosives on it, but there's still one task left to do.

Goat of Warding - Before moving past the Megemycete, there's one last bobblehead goat to destroy in the game. Look to the right of the giant pulsing mass to spot a statue of a woman far off past a pool of black water covered in spiky tendrils. The goat is at the base of the statue, but it can be extremely hard to spot, so you may want to turn your brightness up!

Inside, be sure to check the nearest desk to get a look at reports on all the lords: Dimitrescu's Medical Report, Donna's Medical Report, Moreau's Medical Report, and

Heisenberg's Medical Report. Nearby, there's also a Cadou parasite to inspect, and several photos - including some of Eveline's testing from the previous game.

At the table to the left, you can find a Letter From Spencer File - the man who would go on to create the Umbrella corporation.

Moving around the large center table, there are more photos and Miranda's Diary File to look at, as well as a photo of Miranda and her daughter in a small bookcase nearby. When you're ready, open the nearby cell to get an interesting revelation, and end this sequence.

Boss Battle - Miranda

Important - As you head out onto the Altar site, you'll have one final chance to speak with The Duke. This is your last chance to sell all your treasure, make any food, and buy all the upgrades you can for the rest of the game. Anything you don't sell or finish upgrading will carry over to your next file after completing the game.

Grab some supplies on a crate near The Duke before heading out. To find Miranda, simply take the path of the Lone Road to the Ceremony Site. A few enemies may drop down to hinder you, but you can easily shrug past them until you reach the black mass and push it aside to enter.

Unlike most of the other boss battles, there's no big gimmick to dealing damage this fight. No glowing weak points, no protected hides. Just you, and your final foe. Be sure not to hold anything back with this fight, and unleash all the weapons you have (and craft more ammo as needed).

To her credit, even without super armor Miranda is still a tough enemy to deal with. She will shift between 3 different forms over the course of the fight - her bipedal form, a spider form, and a winged form. On the ground, she'll move around the arena with short dashes before moving her deadly wings in a swipe attack at you. Keep strafing around the arena so you don't give her any direct hits as you let loose with your weapons - it's one of the better times to hit her with slow big guns in this form.

Be sure not to get too close, as she'll also employ a spin attack after her lunges. However, she can summon spiky tendrils - so watch her movements to know when to get out of her way, as they usually erupt in a line in front of her.

When she shifts into a spider-like form, she'll use her sharp new legs to jab at you while moving forward, ending in a bigger lunge that will once again require some quick strafing and dodging.

If she decides to jump onto a nearby ledge, she'll mimic Urias' jump attack, so sprint in another direction to avoid it, then pivot and open fire.

When she takes to the air, she can employ a few different swooping attacks, but that's not the worst of it.

Watch the skies as she dances around for any blobs of megamycete to form around her. If left unchecked, they'll start to glow yellow before bursting into you dealing a lot of damage.

Beat her to the punch by unloading automatic rounds into the blobs as soon as you spot them, and they'll pop harmlessly, letting you get back into the fight. They may also drop ammo for you, making it even better to shoot them quick.

When she moves to the middle and flies up asking for the megamycete's power, she'll begin to form a very big blob above her. Snipe it out of the sky and it will explode onto her, knocking her into the ground.

This will usually be followed by Miranda casting darkness over the arena and vanishing. She'll pop out without warning to move forward and lunge, so keep strafing around the arena and turn as you do to shoot as she lunges past you.

When she takes to the air again, she may summon several tendrils of black writhing roots before summoning an explosive mass in the middle. Use the roots as cover, and you can evade the fire from the middle until it runs its course - and you might be able to aim between the cracks to hit her during the sequence.

As long as you learn the counter moves to all of her attacks, you can stay one step ahead of her, using all your explosives, magnum shots, and rifle rounds to deplete her health.

Eventually, she tries to cover you in the megamycete, holding you in place while she summons a giant blob above you. Since you can't move, unleash all of your ammo into her face with every weapon that still has ammo in it, and out-damage her to win the day.

Rose will now be safe, but even your victory is not without cost. The story will now come to its close, and the megamycete will be detonated, ensuring its power will never be abused again. Congratulations, you've completed your time in The Village!

Once the credits have rolled, you'll be able to save your clear file, and begin New Game+ with all of your weapons, ammo, treasure and money intact for a new run. You'll also unlock Challenges (which retroactively reward you for what you've done so far). This will let you unlock the Mercenaries mode, as well as new weapons and cheats like infinite ammo!

How to Hide From Lady Dimitrescu

Much like Resident Evil 7's Jack Baker or Mr X in the RE2 Remake, Lady Dimitrescu is an unstoppable force that will hound you all through the castle. Thankfully we've got a few tips on how to avoid and escape from the evil giantess and her daughters in Resident Evil Village.

Encountering Lady Dimitrescu

After you arrive in the castle and first meet the lady and her daughters, only one of the three buzzing vampire girls will chase you through the rooms around the Main Hall. Unlike Lady D, you won't be able to hear them coming.

The moment you notice insects start buzzing around you, it's time to run away, since just being near them will slowly drain your health, and shooting them now doesn't really have any effect - so don't waste your ammo!

Luckily they don't move very fast and lose interest after you put a room or two behind you. It's not until you reach Lady Dimitrescu's chambers above the courtyard that she'll begin to hunt you in earnest.

Unlike Jack Baker or Mr. X, your weapons have pretty much no effect on Lady D, and won't even stun her for a short period. Occasionally she'll pause to shrug off some bullet casings, but it's best not to rely on this to slow her down.

She occasionally pauses for a brief moment after extending her claws before performing a lunging swipe attack, but that can deal major damage, so your best use of that time's gonna be to duck around a corner or otherwise out of her line of sight. If you can't get out of the way, timing your block might just be the difference between life and death!

Her massive size can be a problem if you take a wrong turn, so always be sure to plan ahead by checking your map to plan an escape route - if you get caught on the balconies above the Main Hall or Opera Hall, for instance, it's hard to slide past her without taking a lot of damage, so make sure she's nowhere in sight before exploring narrow dead end hallways.

Lady Dimitrescu Hiding Spots

Since running is always the best option, it's good to know where to run to if you need a quick breather from her relentless pursuits. Thankfully, there are several areas she's not fond of going to that you can take advantage of:

- the Merchant's Room where The Duke resides. It's a great spot to plan your next move. Even if she's still wandering around near the Main Hall outside, you can take the side passage near the Entrance Hall to slip past her. In a pinch, you can also duck into the Wine Room above the Main Hall.
- Any rooms leading down to the dungeons, so she won't enter the Kitchen or the upstairs Dressing Room, and she'll stay out of the Hall of Ablution next to her quarters.
- Certain mask rooms are also places she'll avoid, like the Hall of Pleasure, and she'll steer clear of the Library and Hall of Joy - at least until you've claimed the Mask of Joy. After that she'll have no problems chasing you through there
- The Rooftops - locations leading to the attic and top level are places Lady D will avoid. She may use the Hall of Joy, but will always stop at the Atelier where her portrait room is, and won't follow use the Lift to follow you up.

Lady Dimitrescu's Patrol Routes

When she's not actively pursuing you, the towering vampire usually patrols the upper and lower Main Hall, as well as the Opera Hall and adjoining rooms, making it difficult to stay hidden for long.

Her footsteps don't echo as much as Mr X does, but she will very boldly announce herself when she spots you - giving you a heads up that it's time to get moving.

If you've got her on your tail but really need to find a way to keep moving while juking her, the best spots are usually the corridors around the Main Hall, the stairways around the Opera House, and the wide open Courtyard - but just be sure to you take out any enemies who appear around here first.

Her wide swings leave you with little room to run past her, but you CAN block some of her attacks. Even so, it's better to take longer side passages or put a barrier between you and hope her claws can't reach you.

You should also be wary of spending too much time in the Main Hall, as there's always a chance both Lady D and one of her daughters will ambush you around the same time, which is a tag team you absolutely want no part of. Luckily, her daughters never travel farther from the Main Hall than the Dining Room - preferring to stick to the west side of the castle.

How to Open Castle Dimitrescu's Gate

Finding the Maiden Crest

From the large door to Castle Dimitrescu, head right to the church. Moving inside this area, you can head inside to find your first real Save Point, a Typewriter! While you're here, you can claim the first Maiden Crest at the front of a shrine, and you'll notice a large depiction of that framed photo you found earlier, along with 4 other photos which can only be the head honchos of this land. Get a good look at them - this won't be the last you see of them.

Finding the Demon Crest

As for the other crest, look on a nearby chair to spot a map of the village, showing the other crest is nearby at the very same house you heard the radio told you to come to. You can reach it by looking for a path to the right of the church, where a large field separates you from the other house.

The field outside is alive with rustling, as three Lycans are darting through the tall grass. They won't come out in the open however - at least until you either get close enough, or manage to hit them from a distance with your pistol. If you do see them before entering the field, you may want to try luring one out at a time, and either gun them down as they leave the field, or lure them into a mine.

When the enemies have been dealt with, or you choose to run past them, look for a small home to the right of the sealed gate at the top of the field, and enter to find more survivors hiding inside. They are also trying to get to Luiza's house if not for the locked gate. You'll need to help them find a way inside.

Start by hopping out the open window on the other side of the room. You can mantle onto a low platform nearby, then hop through the hole in the wall to reach Luiza's property. Before going inside, note the locked shrine holding the Demon Crest by the gate you can't reach just yet.

Open the gate, and with the help of the villagers you'll be cautiously let inside. While you're told to wait in the front hall for a moment, take the time to save at the Typewriter.

When ready, head down the hall to meet the remaining survivors of the village. Of course, as expected in a Resident Evil game, friendly faces won't be around very long.

When things take a turn for the worse, you'll be attacked but saved by the girl from earlier, and led into a garage area.

The truck works, but is missing its keys. Leave Elena behind and make your way into the next room - where a barricaded door is the only thing between you and freedom.

Ethan will want to ram it with the truck, but you need those keys, so grab them from the bottom drawer in the kitchen.

A nearby note mentions there's something with the key, so inspect it to find a clasp to open and reveal a Screwdriver, which you'll need to get the Demon Crest.

Using the Truck Key, Ethan will try and bust out with limited success. You'll have to climb up to the rafters in the house towards the attic window - but unfortunately Elena won't be joining you.

After the cutscene ends, you can drop out of the window and back to the ground. Use your new Screwdriver to retrieve the Demon Crest.

Be sure to use the Save Point in the Church, then head to the gate and insert both the Maiden Crest and Demon Crest, and turn them until they face the right direction. Once you've done this, the doors will open.

How to Get the Courtyard Key

After the first fight you encounter with one of Dimitrescu's daughters, you'll find yourself in the Kitchen.

While you're here, make sure to grab the Sanguis Virginis from the bloody bowl nearby.

If you went into the Tasting Room on the second floor of the Castle earlier, you'll recall a silver stand on the far wall that's perfectly sized for a bottle of wine. So, head back there.

Go back to the Main Hall and up toward the Tasting Room on the second floor. Place the Sanguis Virginis on its rightful stand to unlock a secret room that holds the Courtyard Key, which can now be used to access the Courtyard.

How to Open Iron Insignia Doors

Finding the Iron Insignia Key

While roaming the Opera Hall in Castle Dimitrescu, you'll come across a piano on the bottom floor. Thankfully, this is a small and easy puzzle.

You need to match the piano keys to the sheet music displayed in order to solve the puzzle.

If you don't read sheet music - not to worry, as pressing a key will show you how close you are to the actual note, and you need only go to the right to go higher, or left to go lower. Once you hit the right note, you'll move onto the next, so you don't have to get all the notes in one flawless string.

Numbering the keys from left to right, the correct sequence is:

*15, 12, 14, 13, 13, 16, 15, 16, 17, 17.

Completing the puzzle will unlock a small slot in the piano that holds the Iron Insignia Key, unlocking even more areas of the castle for you.

Where to use the Iron Insignia Key

The Iron Insignia Key opens a variety of different areas, both in and around the Castle. Below, you'll find a list of each location that can be unlocked with the key.

- Opens the Library door beyond the Opera Hall
- Opens the door to access The Prison Treasure near Castle Dimitrescu
- Opens a gate to a small graveyard behind the church
- Opens a gate near a large house in the village, which gives you access to the Water Wheel
- Opens a locked door in East Old Town, where you can find the GM 79 Grenade Launcher

How to Get The Prison Treasure

Head back down to the prisons and take out any Moroaicas that now wander the dungeons until you reach the locked door, and open it using the Iron Insignia Key.

Inside is a puzzle similar to the other Prison puzzle, but this one can be a bit more annoying to deal with.

There are two swinging braziers - both unlit, guarding a sarcophagus that you can't reach.

In order to light the swinging braziers, look at a cracked wall near the back where a light source is emanating from. Search the nearby walls for a Pipe Bomb and blow open the wall to reveal a large torch.

The difficult part now is using the wonky physics of trying to push a swinging brazier in first person without being able to directly hold it. You can try and push them by running into them, but it's not recommended. If you want a much easier time, you can crouch down and fire a few well placed shots to send the brazier moving much quicker. As long as you're accurate and don't mind wasting several bullets, you can light both the braziers this way - just remember both braziers will need to be swinging towards each other to light up, so you may need to stagger your pushes or shots. Luckily, there's Handgun Ammo both in an alcove and in a crate.

Completing the puzzle will unlock the sarcophagus for you, getting you the Azure Eye Treasure, that can be combined with the Silver Ring you found in the Hall of Pleasure to make the Azure Eye Ring, which sells for much more Lei.

How to Get The Maestro's Collection

Collect Luthier's Key

After you complete your time at House Beneviento and defeat Angie and Donna Beneviento, return to the Garden area near the lift.

You can now head up through a nearby gate on the left to reach the Gardener's House (the same gardener who left a note about the locked house in the Village).

Inside the house is a Save Point, Luthier's Key to the village house, a Gardener's Diary File by the bed, and some Explosive Rounds.

Unlock Luthier's Door to the Maestro's Collection

Now that you have obtained Luthier's Key from the Gardener's Shack near House Beneviento, you can now return to West Old Town and unlock the door for it. The house is located near the house with a red chimney.

The main treasure here is located in a cabinet with a combination lock, so you'll need to look around for clues. There's a paper with the model number of a violin - but ignore that and instead look on the same table for a scrap of paper that says "I will never forget her fifth birthday".

Head to the kitchen and look in the corner to spot a small happy birthday drawing with a date on it: 27, 09, 17. Input it into the combination lock, and you'll find both a Steel Hraesvelgr treasure and a chest with an F2 Rifle - High-Capacity Mag, which you can combine into your rifle!

How to Get The Waterwheel Weapon

With the newly upgraded Winged Key, it's time to finally head back to East Old Town where you got attacked by that giant Lycan with the hammer. He's not around anymore, but unfortunately, a new enemy is, and wastes no time practically mauling Ethan to death.

The werewolf beast known as the Varcolac is a terrifying foe, and can deal major damage quickly, so you'll need to run and gun and do your best to focus on surprise attacks before retreating into buildings.

The fight will start as it tosses you into the building, and as long as you keep some distance, you'll find it can't actually enter (but will swipe wide into the rooms you hide in), so either unload with the shotgun, or quickly climb to the roof as it loses track of you. There's also a dead body in the building holding Vasile's Final Testament File, which mentions getting to the nearby watermill.

Big impact weapons like the Rifle and Shotgun work well here for damage, as will Pipe Bombs and Mines - but it can be hard to stagger. However, if it does loose track of you and starts wandering away to the south, you may want to quickly drop down and run to the edge of the stream where a locked door can finally be opened with the Iron Insignia Key.

Inside is the GM 79 Grenade Launcher, a weapon that can launch explosive projectiles - ammo you may already have a few of by this point.

How to Get Luiza's Heirloom

Return to Luiza's House

After returning to the Village once you have completed Castle Dimitrescu, there are certain spots that have changed with new enemies and treasures.

Now will be a great time to return to the Fallow Plot to see what's become of Luiza's house. Three winged Samcas circle the place, so you may want to snipe a few before they reach you. Another hides in the tall grass, so be sure to advance cautiously and avoid their lunges from the air.

Luiza's house is still a smoking wreck, but items have been placed around the entrance, including Luiza's Heirloom in a small box.

Be sure to carefully inspect Luiza's Heirloom in your menu. As it turns out, you can interact with the necklace to remove the Necklace Stone to sell for 8,000 Lei. Even more important is inspecting the remaining necklace to find Luiza's Key hidden inside.

This can be used to finally unlock a small chest in the room back on the Lone Path outside the Altar, which contains Cesare's Goblet, worth 19,000 Lei.

How to Get Beneviento's Treasure

Beneviento's Treasure Location

Making your way to the Garden towards House Beneviento for the first time, Ethan will begin to see visions as you progress.

You'll end up in a large gravesite with a large headstone for a member of the Beneviento family, but part of the slab with their name is missing. You won't be able to access it until after you have defeated Donna and Angie and returned to The Village.

Locate the Missing Slab

For this optional treasure, you're going to want to make sure you have a lot of ammo, especially explosive types, and a few First Aid Med, as the treasure won't be given up without a fight.

Head to the Village's graveyard above the Maiden of War statue, and you'll find along with some new ghouls, a small mausoleum has opened, allowing you to pick up a Broken Slab. This is the same slab that was missing from the large Beneviento tombstone past the garden.

Defeat the Giant Guarding the Gravestone

When you reach the large tombstone, be ready. A giant wielding an even more giant axe will crash into the area signaling a miniboss fight. This large hulking enemy can deal a ton of damage with just a single swing, so you'll want to be ready to dodge at a moment's notice.

Beyond his slow and powerful overhead swings, this giant can and will leap across the entire arena if you put too much distance between you.

If the giant moves his weapon back into a stance, you'll need to be careful. It will either be a low stance with his weapon behind him, or holding his axe high. Either method will have the giant slowly advance upon you, and if it closes the distance, the giant will unleash a large sweeping strike that will deal major damage.

If that wasn't bad enough, the giant will also summon a few Moroaicas from time to time to help him during the fight. Depending on your ammo count, you may want to consider dodging around them as they move fairly slowly - but it's better to employ explosives to damage all of them when they move close together, so the Moroaicas can go down while you damage the giant. Luckily, the Moroaicas tend to drop lots of crafting resources, allowing you to stay in the fight longer by making more healing items or ammo.

Try to aim for the head after the giant swings or jumps and stays vulnerable for a bit, but always be ready to sprint away at a moment's notice. It will take a lot of firepower to bring it down, so if you're having trouble, you may want to come back later.

Collect Beneviento's Treasure

Should you defeat the giant, you'll gain a Giant Crystal Axe that sells for a 30,000 Lei, and if that wasn't enough, you can now put the Broken Slab at the foot of the tombstone, and it will reveal Berengario's Chalice which also sells for 18,000 Lei!

How to Get Moreau's Hidden Weapon

After you've taken the lift back up the first mill with the Labyrinth puzzle, you'll find that you can now open the mechanical gate on the right using the Crank. Going up the mountain path, you'll find a fork - and it's best you go up the upper right path first to find a crate, and a bridge over to a small shrine that holds the Mermaid Ball needed for the

Labyrinth back down below. Turning around, you can spot two Winged Creatures flying around the two nearby buildings, with a third perched on a high hill nearby. Be sure to snipe one or two of them and then sneak up on the one perched at the top.

Cautiously advance into the two large buildings between the giant pile of dead beasts, and you'll find a few Ghouls inside to kill. As you head up to the third building on the small hill, you can probably hear the sounds of something inside. Move around to the back of the building to find a small hole to crawl through, allowing you to get the drop on the Lycan by the door and blow off his head.

Read Moreau's Diary of Experiments File on the desk, and then open the nearby chest to find the coveted M1851 Wolfsbane Revolver a true powerhouse of a weapon.

How to Get to the Riverbank Treasure House

The following treasure location can only be accessed once you have obtained the Crank while exploring the Reservoir area, and defeated Salvatore Moreau.

From the Altar, start making your way back to the Ceremony Site by traveling along the Lone Road, but stop at the large bridge. If you go down to the right, you can lower the drawbridge on the side using your new Crank you obtained at the Reservoir from Moreau. Cross the drawbridge and you'll find a crate and a boat you can use to ride up and down the river.

Start by taking the boat north towards Castle Dimitrescu. While you can't re-enter the castle here, you can disembark at a small dock and lower a crank back to the Craftsman's Hut outside the Tower of Worship.

Use the Crank to Descend Into the Well

Be sure to head into the back of the shack and open the outhouse for Gunpowder if you missed it last time, and to use the Well Wheel to dredge up the well and find... a ladder down?

Descend into the well and look in the puddles of water to find a Lockpick, and then move forward to find a room full of hanging spike traps. They won't fall on you, but there's a puzzle to solve if you want to get what's behind the locked gate at the far end.

Start by grabbing a Mine on the right, then move towards the locked gate, and climb up onto the raised platform on the right, and up to another raised platform to reach a ledge. There's a Pipe Bomb here, but more importantly is a control panel that raises and lowers a few of the spike traps.

Hit the two white lights to bring up both platforms at the far end up - including the one with the minecart on it. Cross to the other side and grab some '''Shotgun Ammo''' along the rocks, and then push the nearby cart forward until you can reach the minecart on the platform, and then push it off down below. This will create a platform to get you over to the ledge with the crate you can break.

Now, drop down into the hole, and open the chest for a Large Pigeon Blood Ruby, and look under the torture rack for Flashbangs and Magnum Ammo. Unlocking the door will pull up all the spike trap platforms - but don't worry, they won't be coming down again.

Light the Torches in the Treasure Hold

Back across the drawbridge, look for a door with torches on the side to enter a treasure hold. This secret area features two unlit torches with a swinging brazier in the middle, and a second unlit torch in the far room, along with a crate.

To unlock solve the Riverbank Treasure House puzzle, start by lighting the two torches in the first room. While you can try your luck at pushing, it's much easier to crouch down behind the brazier to angle your pistol shot upward so the brazier swings hard into the torch - then do the same for the other side.

The doors will unlock as the torches are lit - the one on the left holds a treasure trove of Lei, while the other door has a few crates, and a hole in the wall that a Ghoul will start crawling out of. At this point you'll notice two things: The second room with the torch can't be reached by the swinging brazier, and killing the ghoul will only make a new one crawl out.

Putting two and two together, you'll need to use the Ghoul as a flammable guinea pig. Let him stumble after you into the brazier room and push it into his face, lighting the poor guy on fire.

This won't kill him outright, so you can have the burning zombie chase you into the next room, and make him lunge at the torch to open the final room - then kill him.

Inside you'll find the grand treasure - the Golden Lady Statue, which is worth 20,000 Lei when sold to The Duke.

How to Get Cannibal's Plunder

On the path to the Stronghold, use the Six Wing Unborn Key, but take the left path at the last "Good Luck" sign to come out onto a large lumber mill.

Ignore the explosive barrels in the river for now, and instead start exploring outside.

Since the door on the right side of the mill is locked, cross the stream to the far side, then head inside the mill.

A loud scream will ring out as you enter, followed by loud thudding noises. As you move into the main mill room, you'll find out why.

Another giant enemy with an equally giant axe - the same as the one from the garden graveyard - makes his home here, and he does not like intruders.

Unlike the other giant fight, you'll have a lot more room to maneuver here. This is good, because the giant will employ a lot of sweeping attack, especially when he holds his axe in a low sweeping stance or high overhead stance. He can and will also jump great distances to strike down on you, so you should constantly be on the move as you fight this enemy.

Use everything in your disposal to slow him down - plant mines, toss pipe bombs, and use explosive rounds when he's standing still, and make use of the ammo scattered around the mill.

At certain points he'll call out for backup, but there won't be ghouls this time. Instead, he'll summon Winged Creatures to help him fight.

This is actually not as bad as it sounds, as these enemies usually dart around for a long time before attacking, and you can usually either catch them with an explosive blast from your weapons, or quickly turn and fill them with shotgun shells to kill them quickly.

There are also two red barrels you can utilize both to interrupt the giant, and tear apart any friends he has at the same time.

Remember that the Winged Creatures will also drop even more crafting resources should you start to run low on ammo. He's pretty vulnerable when calling for help, so take that time to unload some sniper rifle shots on his face, or hit him point blank with a shotgun a few times before running away.

When the giant axe man finally falls, gather his Giant Crystal Axe and slice open all three padlocks on the far door. Make sure you've cleaned the place out for ammo and head into the next room.

In the cannibal's storehouse, you can find a ton of meat to give to the Duke, including 3 Meat, 1 Poultry, and 1 Fish Meat.

The room also has an Herb to replenish your health, as well as Metal Scrap, and Ernest's Diary File on the table.

Finally, enter the last room to find a small table with a chest holding the real prize - Father Nichola's Angel, which sells for 22,000 Lei to The Duke.

How to Get The Treasure Under the Stronghold

Following the mini boss fight with Urias and the brief interaction with Heisenberg, head out of this chamber and pass through the next hall. Here, you'll find Guglielmo's Plate on the left before taking the small boat up the underground stream to dock not far away - with a ladder heading topside to the cemetery behind the church.

This treasure sells to The Duke for 25,000 Lei.

How to Get the Relief of a Horse

Find the Relief Mold

Inside the Foundry, there's a large Casting Machine against the far wall that will be central to solving a few puzzles in the Factory.

You can't interact with a strange hole in the wall, and another door is locked, leaving only one way out of the room for now. Going up the hall, three more ghouls are stumbling around a walkway, and can be bunched up nicely for an explosion to send them flying. Note the unpowered switch for a door, forcing you towards a far door into a lab area.

In here, there's a creepy body with a drill for an arm in the next room, and if you think it's going to jump out and grab you - you might be right! Move past the body for now into the next room and open a chest that has a Relief Mold you can use back in the Foundry.

As expected, the enemy known as the Soldat will power up off his chair and move to attack. These enemies are extremely sturdy and can block shots with their drill arm, and deal some major damage if you get hit. Luckily, they move fairly slow, and take a few moments to swing or stab with their main weapon - which also leaves the large red light on their chest vulnerable to attack.

Get some distance on them using the nearby hallways and goad them into attacking then sprint away, pivot, and ready your rifle to zero in on their weak points. Dealing enough damage will short circuit them out, killing them instantly, and rewarding you with a Crystal Mechanical Heart.

Create the Relief of a Horse

Back in the Foundry, place the Relief Mold in the Casting Machine to obtain a Relief of a Horse, which you can then place on the hole in the wall behind you.

How to Get the Cog Mold

After opening the passage with the Relief of a Horse, continue forward until you drop down into the large Engine Room downstairs. Then, take a look at the large engine machines that dot the zig-zagging walkway through this room.

The giant pistons here will move back and forth rapidly, swinging in front of the narrow parts of each walkway - and can damage you relentlessly if you move slowly beneath them. If you are worried sprinting won't be enough, you can shoot the red dots on each piston to stop them and give you safe passage - but you'll still have to worry about the ghouls up ahead.

You can actually take a few potshots at the enemies on the far side with your pistol, which will cause them to slowly stumble around to find you, and most likely get them killed trying to get past the large damaging pistons. Three more will appear in the middle section once you cross, so you'll either have to quickly sprint back, or fight them head on without the help of the pistons.

When all enemies are dead, you can blow out the remaining pistons to travel safely across. Look for the final piston's red light on the wall behind it and carefully snipe it to access a ladder taking you back upstairs.

Crawl through the vent. The door next to you is locked, so instead you'll have to move down the hall full of Soldats just waiting to come alive - but they won't…. Yet. Head through and unlock the door back to the Foundry before moving further down the stairs in the previous room. There's a cracked wall here, but you can leave it for now as you explore the rest of the room to find a breakable crate and a backup generator missing a gear.

Downstairs are a number of fences. Going up the stairs to the right, you'll find a door with red lights you can smash to enter.

In this storeroom, check on the left for a Development Note 1 File on a table, and a Factory Map (Lower Levels) to the right by some Gunpowder. Open the large case by the file to get the Cog Mold, and unlock the far door to get back into the hall full of Soldats.

How to Complete the Necklace With Two Holes

Once you have the Well Wheel, head to the well behind the church to lift up the bucket inside. Here, you'll find a Necklace with Two Holes. This is only part of a Treasure that can eventually be sold to The Duke, however, it also requires two gems to be fully complete.

These gems are the Pigeon Blood Ruby and Large Pigeon Blood Ruby. The former can be found close by in East Old Town, so head there first.

Behind one of the houses, which you'll need the Crank to access, you'll find a ladder that you can take up onto the cliffs. Follow it along to the roof of a shed, where you'll find the Pigeon Blood Ruby in a small chest.

The next gem is found near the river, so head back towards the Ceremony Site and drop down near the bridge. Use your Crank again so it goes down, then cross over and take the boat up river.

Once you reach the dock, disembark and head left. You'll find another bridge that you'll have to bring down using your Crank. Then, cross over to find the Craftsman's Hut again. Head back inside and through the back window to the well.

With your Well Wheel in hand, you'll notice a ladder come up that you can take down. So, follow it down into the well below. From here, head into the room behind you and you'll have a puzzle to solve.

Climb up onto the raised platform on the right, and up to another raised platform to reach a ledge. There's a control panel here that raises and lowers a few of the spike traps.

Hit the two white lights to bring up both platforms at the far end up - including the one with the minecart on it. Cross to the other side and then push the nearby cart forward until you can reach the minecart on the platform, and then push it off down below. This will create a platform to get you over to the ledge with the crate you can break.

Now, drop down into the hole, and open the small chest for the Large Pigeon Blood Ruby. You can combine both gems with the Necklace now, creating Dimitrescu's Necklace, which sells for 50,000 Lei to The Duke.

Looking for even more on Resident Evil Village? Check out our complete Walkthrough, our comprehensive How-To Guides, and our detailed Puzzle Solutions that will help guide you through every step of the way.

How to Get the Well Wheel

Use the Iron Insignia key on the gate near the red chimney house on the street. Here, you'll find the Well Wheel in a shack. With this key item, you can now raise up all the wells around the village to collect various items!

Here are the different wells that you can use the Well Wheel on in and around the village:
- The well to the right of the Maiden of War statue holds the Wooden Animal (Head) Treasure that can be combined with the Wooden Animal (Body) to sell for greater profit.
- The well behind the Church holds a Necklace with Two Holes that seems to have room 2 gems.

- The well behind the first house in West Old Town has one Lockpick
- The well next to Luiza's House has 3 Pipebombs
- The well near the Gardener's Shack by House Beneviento holds the Madalina (Head)
- The well near where you find the Mermaid Ball in The Reservoir holds Flashbangs
- The well by the Craftsman's Hut near Castle Dimitrescu brings up a ladder that leads you to a treasure trove of goods, including a Lockpick, Mine, Pipe Bomb, Magnum Ammo, Flashbangs, and the Large Pigeon Blood Ruby

How to Pick Locks

The only way to open these specific drawers and cabinets in Resident Evil Village is by using a one-time use Lockpick, which are rare items found by exploring the village and areas beyond.

Not only are Lockpicks hard to come by, but the locations of locked drawers may not be reached once you move onto other areas of Resident Evil Village, and so finding Lockpicks early can help you pick every lock you come across.

Lockpick Locations

There is a finite amount of Lockpicks that you can find in Resident Evil Village, and below you will find the locations of each lockpick and locked item.

There are 10 Lockpicks to find in the game, but only 8 locked drawers you need to use them on, so if you don't find all the Lockpicks, you can still get all the goods!

Note that after completing the game, and starting a new game from your completed file, all of your inventory items will carry over, including any Lockpicks that you did not use.

Lockpick Locations	
Castle Dimitrescu	On a table between the Kitchen and Dining Room
	Armory - in the back of the room next to some Pipe Bombs
	Attic - On a table in the corner guarded by an enemy
The Village	Inside the outhouse next to the Maestro's (Luthier's) home, across from the Iron Insignia Gate
	Inside a well behind the first house in West Old Town, dredged up using the Water Wheel
	In the Waterwheel house locked by the Iron Insignia, on a windowsill near the GM 79 Grenade Launcher

	Inside the well behind the Craftsman's Hut (return via the riverboat after getting the Crank), in a puddle at the bottom of the well's ladder
House Beneviento	Inside the Garden Shack near the W870 TAC Shotgun
Heisenberg's Factory	At the end of the tunnel with the large drill embedded in the ground on floor B3, in a cabinet on the left side of the room.
	Inside the Operating Room back on floor B4 once the door is powered by the backup generator, on a desk on the left as you enter

Locked Drawer Locations and Contents

Area	*Location*	*Contents*
Castle Dimitrescu	Hallway between Kitchen and Dining Room	Wooden Angel Statue
	Room leading to Bedchamber	Shotgun Ammo
	Upper Opera Hall, at the end of the right hallway	Sniper Rifle Ammo
The Village	First House you enter in the Village	Sniper Rifle Ammo
	House to the left of the Maiden of War Statue (near the first Crone encounter)	Shotgun Ammo
	House to the right of the Maiden of War Statue (opens up on second visit)	Shotgun Ammo
Heisenberg's Factory	Cabinet in the corner of hallway leading to Operating Room (powered door)	Yellow Quartz
	Drawer outside the door to Heisenberg's Quarters on floor B4, above the Engine Room	Magnum Ammo

How to Unlock Infinite Ammo

Once you have beaten the game for the first time, you will unlock Challenges and the Extra Content Shop. Completing challenges will earn you Challenge Points (CP), which can then be used to purchase various types of content - including Infinite Ammo.

Please Note - in order to unlock infinite ammo for a chosen weapon, you must first purchase all weapon modifications and upgrade its components to the maximum at The

Duke's Emporium, and only then can you purchase the infinite ammo cheat in the Extra Content Shop. However, certain weapons, like the Grenade Launcher, do not have upgrades, and infinite ammo can be purchased for them by default.

If you want to unlock Infinite Ammo for a weapon but don't mind not having it fully upgraded, there's a trick to quickly unlocking inifinte ammo for multiple weapons. Accumulate as much treasure as possible during a run, and when you start a New Game+ file, save next to The Duke and sell everything except the gun you wish to upgrade fully. Once its upgraded, reload the save file and fully upgrade another weapon - as the infinite ammo will be unlocked for the previous weapon.

List of Infinite Ammo Cheat Unlocks

Weapon Name	*Infinite Ammo CP Cost*
LEMI Handgun	10,000 CP
M1911 Handgun	40,000 CP
V61 Custom Handgun	60,000 CP
M1897 Shotgun	20,000 CP
W870 TAC Shotgun	50,000 CP
SYG-12 Shotgun	70,000 CP
F2 Sniper Rifle	80,000 CP
GM 79 Grenade Launcher	80,000 CP
M1851 Wolfsbane Magnum	95,000 CP
S.T.A.K.E. Magnum	120,000 CP
Handcannon PZ Magnum	90,000 CP
WCX Rifle	60,000 CP
USM-AI Handgun	40,000 CP
Dragoon Rifle	50,000 CP
Rocket Pistol	

Tips and Tricks

Get Every Advantage in Combat

Resident Evil Village will often throw small groups of enemies at you, and unlike the shambling zombies of games past, lycans move in quick to stalk, strafe, and lunge at you.

Make sure you utilize everything around you to even the playing field - look for shelves to push in front of openings or bags of flour you can hit to blind opponents, giving you more time to get off precise shots on distracted foes.

Many enemies can wield weapons that will deal even more damage than usual - but you can shoot them in the leg to knock them down and give yourself a bit of breathing room, or permanently disarm them with a shot to the arm.

Ethan's new combat training means you can not only block incoming attacks, but briefly holding block when an enemy strikes - instead of just tapping the button - will stop their advance for a moment, allowing you to tap the block button once more to push the enemy back, which usually stuns them just long enough to line up a headshot.

If you're having trouble aiming, try adjusting the settings for camera and aim acceleration in the options menu. It will feel different for each person, but we found turning it all the way off makes aiming accurately much easier.

Explore Everywhere

Yellow is the most important color in Village. Not only does it signify interactive objects, it can also help point the way forward or to helpful items and areas - so keep your eyes peeled. Breakable crates, ladders, switches, even birdcages will all have splashes of yellow, and if you see a yellow rope on the ground, it may lead you to pools of water with fish you can hunt.

Making the Most of Inventory Space

Your inventory works a bit differently than in previous Resident Evil games. While it's similar in style to RE 4, you don't have to worry about juggling keys or crafting components. With this in mind, grab every gunpowder, herb, and resource you can find - if you're worried about running out of actual inventory space, just wait until you need to heal or reload to start crafting.

Speaking of inventory management, you'll eventually find alternate pistols and shotguns to use. If you like one variant over the other, don't be afraid to sell it to The Duke to make a tidy sum and free up some space. He'll even pay more if you've upgraded it a bit first.

That said, if you are going to sell your extra pistol or shotgun, be sure not to waste ammo by using up the entire clip first before swapping to your new weapon. Every bullet counts!

One thing that does take up inventory space is animal and fish meat you can start harvesting a little ways into the game. You can unlock permanent upgrades from The Duke with enough ingredients, but the good news is he doesn't need all the ingredients at once, so offload your meats to him often to free up room.

Know the Real Worth of Treasure

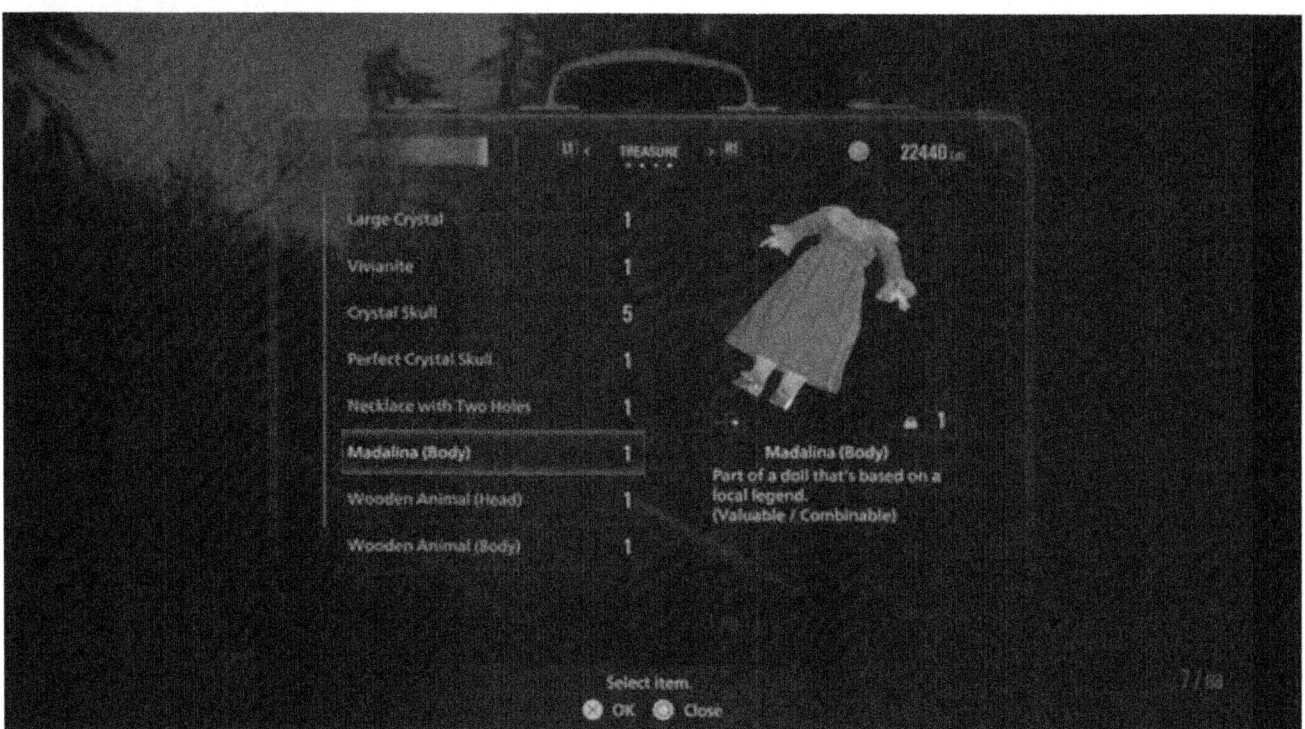

There's a lot of treasure to be found in Village, but be sure to take a moment to inspect it all. Sometimes treasure can be combined to increase its value by a huge amount, so it's worth waiting until you find the other part before combining and selling it as one item.

Some treasure can be harder to spot than others, so be sure to inspect the environment carefully. If you see a glowing spot on a wall or ceiling, shoot it down to collect valuable crystals. You can also listen for the faint creaking noise of bird cages twisting in the wind to shoot them down from the trees.

Enjoy Your Stay in The Village

You'll be returning to the Village itself several times over the course of your adventure, but it will be at least a little different each time. Be sure to revisit previously explored areas to find new enemies, animals, and pathways to travel that you weren't there before.

Unlike the bulk of the Village, there are certain contained areas of the game you won't be able to return to for various reasons. Some are small like Luiza's house in the village, and others can include much larger regions - we won't list them all here for obvious spoiler reasons, but always be sure to make one last sweep of an area before leaving to get any last hidden treasures, or you may miss out on some good loot that will be forever out of your reach.

Resident Evil Village crystal fragments, treasure locations, and how to get more money fast

Resident Evil Village crystal fragments, along with Treasures are a good way to make money fast at the start of the game. At the beginning, money, called Lei in the game, is at premium if you want upgrades and useful stuff from the... resident merchant, the Duke. As by some miracle, this guy is able to set up shop in the strangest of places throughout the game, so you will frequently be tempted to buy a useful upgrade or an epic new weapon.

Of course, the Duke is not here for charity. You need plenty of Resident Evil Village's currency, Lei, to buy the things you want. And knowing how to make a whole lot of money early can make a real difference. So here we've a list of different ways to make money in the early stages of Resident Evil Village. Ranging from early Resident Evil Village crystal fragments to the most valuable treasures, here's how you get your hands on a huge stack of Lei.

How to make money in Resident Evil Village

There are several ways to earn Lei in Resident Evil Village. The most obvious one is by picking up small bags of money from barrels or enemy drops. Even better than these coin pouches, are the crystal skulls and other types of crystal loot drops. They won't drop as frequently, but they're worth far more Lei when you sell them to the Duke.

Besides that, you can keep an eye out for little sparkles. If you see one of these small, flickering white lights, you can bet there's a crystal fragment or other type of gem there. These crystals are usually out of reach (think of walls, statues, ceilings), but they will fall down once you shoot them.

Finally, there's the option of collecting Resident Evil's many treasures. You can often find them in ornate chests, in locked rooms, or just waiting for you in plain sight. Beware that some of these treasures are combinable. Hover over them before selling to see if there's a missing part. If they can be combined, find the other part(s) first to make sure you get the best price possible!

Use these Resident Evil Village crystal fragments locations to earn some fast cash

You can find Resident Evil Village crystal fragments right after entering the village. Every crystal fragment can be exchanged for 2000 Lei at the Duke's shop, so this is well worth your while. Take a look at these maps to see where you can find Resident Evil Village crystal fragments almost as soon as you get started:

Resident Evil Village crystal fragments, main Village

- Crystal Fragment 1: The Maiden of War statue on the Village's main square. The crystal fragment is behind her shield.
- Crystal Fragment 2: Inside the church. See the collection of pictures on the wooden ceiling in front of the altar? The middle one contains a crystal fragment.

Resident Evil Village crystal fragments locations in Castle Dimitrescu

There's also a bunch of Resident Evil Village crystal fragments throughout Castle Dimitrescu that will help you out if you can find them all. You can find nine in total as you progress through the castle which will leave you 18, 000 Lei richer, and help fund your monster fighting Euro tour. Here's where to find them all:

Resident Evil Village crystal fragments locations, Castle Dimitrescu 1F

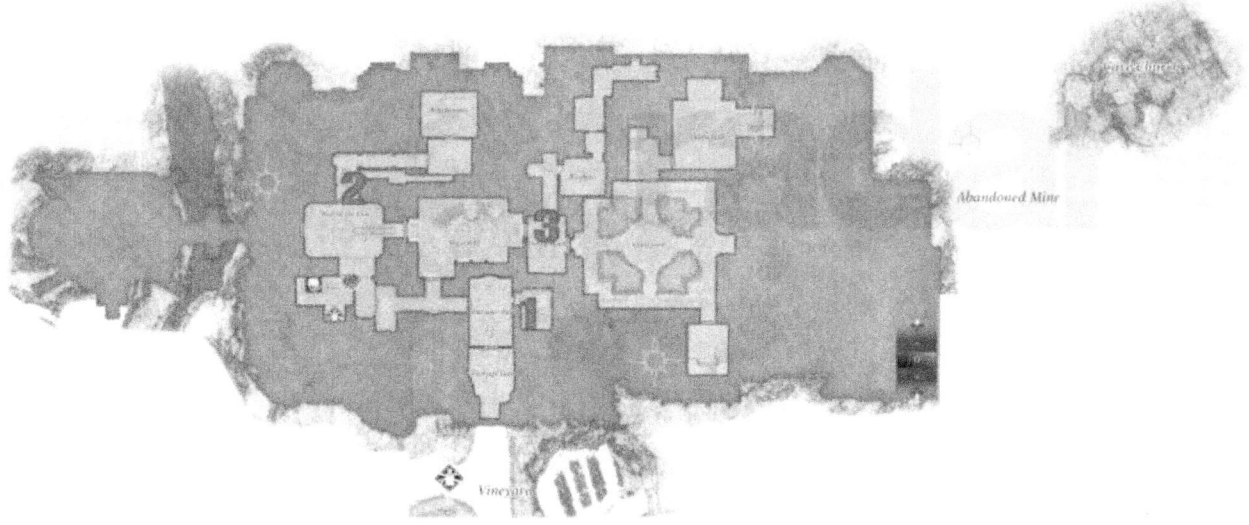

- Crystal Fragment 1: In the room east of the Entrance Hall. Turn your back to the elevator and look up; you'll see the crystal high above you on the wall.
- Crystal Fragment 2: When walking from Lady Dimitrescu's Bedchamber to the Hall of the Four, you'll see a glass cupboard at the end of the narrow hallway (on your left). Smash the glass with your knife to grab the crystal fragment.
- Crystal Fragment 3: On the north side of the Dining Room, right in the middle of the circle on the ceiling.

Resident Evil Village crystal fragments locations, Castle Dimitrescu 2F

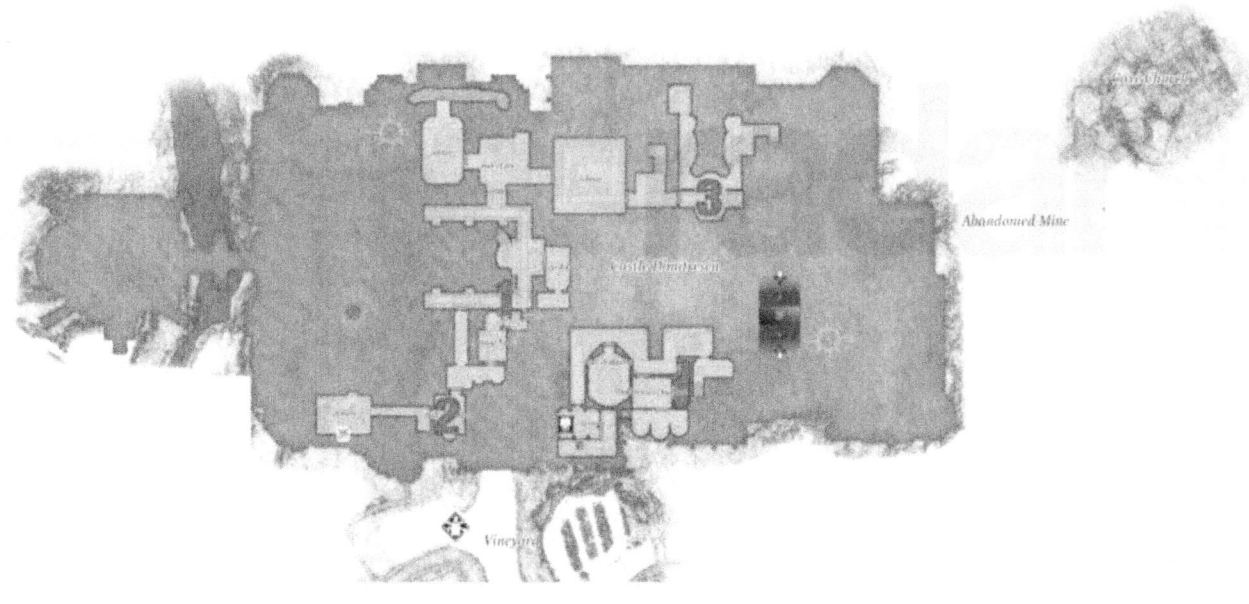

- Crystal Fragment 1: On the ceiling in the passageway between the Tasting Room and the Hall of War.
- Crystal Fragment 2: In the Special Chambers. You can get it by using the Iron Insignia Key when you have it and blowing up the left wall of the room (with a pipe bomb). The crystal is lying on a wooden box.

Resident Evil Village crystal fragments locations, Castle Dimitrescu RF

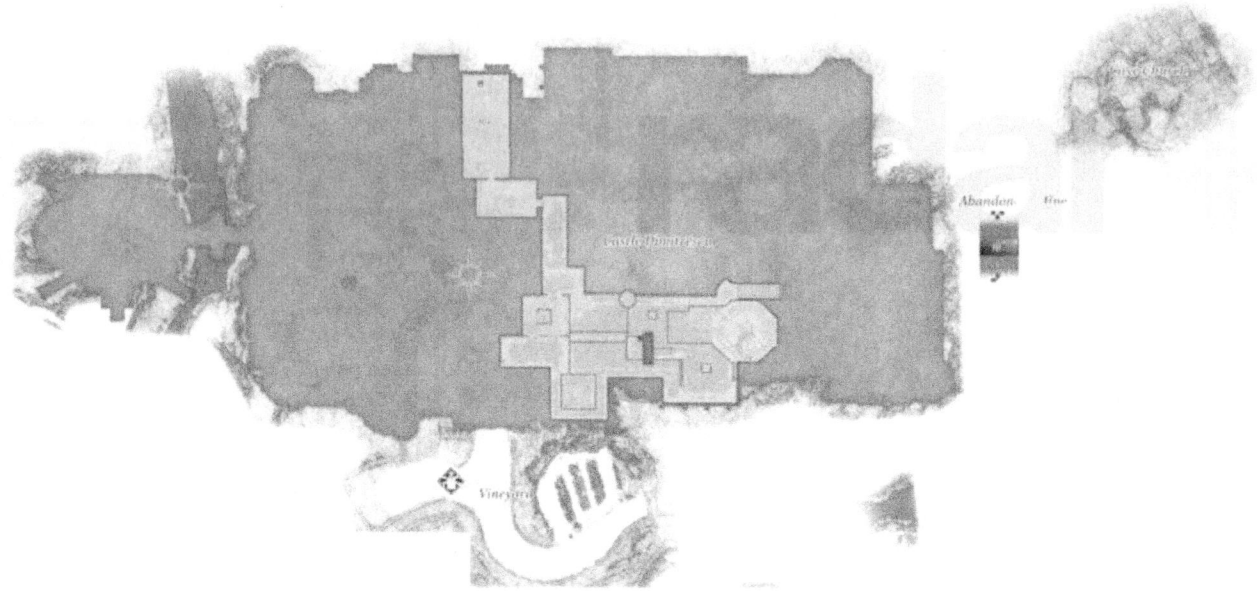

Finally, there's a crystal fragment to be found on Castle Dimitrescu's roof:

- Crystal Fragment 1: On the Castle's roof. Look at the east side of the tower; it's just above the window.

Where to find Resident Evil Village treasures

The Village and Castle Dimitrescu are home to lots of hidden Resident Evil Village treasures. Again, finding them sooner rather than later can help you a lot. If you don't want to miss them, make sure you check whether a room is red or blue on the map before you leave. If it's red, there may still be some valuables inside. Best to have another look!

To help you on your way, here are some of the easiest and most valuable treasures to get in Castle Dimitrescu right at the start of the game:

- Before you leave Lady Dimitrescu's Bedchamber, be sure to grab that beautiful Crimson Glass from her bedside table. This is one of the easiest treasures to get, and it fetches no less than 3500 Lei.
- Ingrid's Necklace. Remember how to set the undead on fire in the Hall of War? One of them will drop Ingrid's Necklace. Priced at 2000 Lei, this is not the most valuable treasure in Castle Dimitrescu, but it's relatively easy to get.
- The Crimson Skull. This item can be sold for 8000 Lei, and what's more: it's located

right next to the Duke in the Merchant's Room. You need to get the Flower Swords Ball in the northwestern corner of the Opera Hall first, and then complete the labyrinth in the Merchant's Room to receive it.
- There's a combinable treasure that is worth 12,000 Lei if you find both parts. You'll find a Silver Ring in a cabinet inside the Hall of Pleasures, when you're tracking down masks, that has a slot for something to be added. Once you receive the Iron Insignia Key you can unlock the treasure you need inside the Special Chamber in the northeastern corner of the castle B1 level. Blow a hole in the wall to expose the torch and light all the fires to gain access to the tomb and receive the Azure Eye. Combine it with the Silver Ring and sell it for that big pay out.

Kill more enemies at the start to get crystal skulls and other loot you can sell for cash

Early on in the game combat might seem scary, but all the minor enemies you fight have a chance to drop a crystal skull in their remains. They're not the most valuable things you can pick up but are easy to accumulate and quickly add cash to your reserves. These are some of the best places to get valuable crystal loot drops early on in Resident Evil Village:

- During the first major lycan attack in the Village. Although this might go a bit against your survival instinct, try to kill as many of them as you can.
- Kill all the undead in the Chamber of Solace in the Castle (basement 1). Again, you may not feel entirely comfortable doing this, especially as there are a great many of them. However, on your way in, you will come across a puzzle involving a fire (Hall of War). When the undead start chasing you, just walk all the way back and watch on as they burn. Now you just need to pick up the loot!
- Defeating Lady Dimitrescu's daughters. You have to face them anyway but as their drops are very valuable and easy to get early in the game though, they deserve a spot on this list. Sell their crystal torsos at the Duke's for a high amount of Lei.

Resident Evil Village - how to survive the attack at the start

How to survive the attack at the start of Resident Evil Village isn't clear. The objective seems simple, but your'e outnumbered and it's easy to die. This is your first big combat encounter and it really throws you in the deep end. There is a trick, however, in knowing how to survive the attack at the start of Resident Evil Village. And once you understand what's really going on you'll be able to literally live to fight another day.

How to survive the attack in Resident Evil Village

The real trick to surviving the attack in Resident Evil Village is to understand that you're not meant to take out all the werewolves. It's a timed moment and when the clock is up a bell will ring and trigger a cut scene. Whatever you try to do, at a certain time you'll be grabbed and thrown to a specific area to watch all the creatures react to the bell and wander off.

So, you'll have just as much success running away as you will trying to fight. Keep moving in loops to avoid getting hemmed in and you'll stand a much better chance. play with:

Grab the shotgun, and use the house

Head into the house and you'll find a shotgun on the table inside, which will give you a firepower boost as long as your ammo lasts. There's also some handgun ammo, gunpowder and a herb in there. This house is also a handy way to bottleneck enemies - you can hide in the porch and deal with them one at a time to last longer. Or, if you want to stay more mobile, there's a ladder in a back room you can use to get out under the floor - gather the lycans in the house, then leave through the hole in the floor where they can't follow to buy some time.

User the barrel to take a few enemies out

If you can get here on the map you'll find a red barrel that will explode when you shoot it. If you can cluster enemies up around it you can take a bunch out. The risk being that you're backing yourself into a corner. However the blast will knock most nearby lycans over, even if it doesn't kill them, so you'll have a window to escape with.

Basically, hang tight, try not to get killed and being able to survive the attack in Resident Evil Village is basically a case of waiting it out. When the bell rings and the bad things go away you'll be free to carry on with the rest of the game.

Resident Evil Village statue puzzle solution

The Resident Evil Village statue puzzle in the Hall of Ablution asks you to arrange some statues according to a poem on the wall. It's a classic Resident Evil test, and if you want to know how to solve it and get everything in its right place, we have the answer here. This is a critical path puzzle and you won't be able to progress until you've done it. Once completed you'll be able to carry on with the story and see what else is in store.

Resident Evil Village statue puzzle solution

The solution to this puzzle is on the wall at the back on a plaque that reads:

"Women are blind to male advances, but the poor shall take their chances to give their lord their bounty sown, so soon the wine may flow."

If you look at the back of the statues you'll get a prompt you can use to turn them either left of right. The poem is basically a coded message as to how you should face each one to continue. Assuming you haven't turned all the statues all over the place, you only need to turn three of the four statues to complete this challenge.

"Women are blind to male advances..."

There are two female statues on the left hand side of the room if you're facing away from the plaque. When you first enter they will be facing the men on the other side of the room. Simply turn them to face each other.

"...but the poor shall take their chances to give their lord their bounty sown"

There are three men on the right hand side of the room (facing away from the plaque) offering up a plate of food. Simply turn them to face the 'lord' rearing up on the horse.

"...so soon the wine may flow."

And that's the puzzle done. You don't have to touch the guy on the horse at all. As soon as the two ladies are facing each other, and the three men are facing the statue on horseback, the pool will drain and you'll be able to carry on down the stairs that are revealed.

Resident Evil Village piano puzzle solution - how to press the right keys

The Resident Evil Village Piano puzzle is a test you face in Castle Dimitrescu where you have to play some sheet music, press some keys and aim for the right notes. Although you don't know why, which means you can poke a few keys, not get it, and move on. However, you need to solve the Resident Evil Piano puzzle to progress for reasons that will become abundantly clear in a moment.

So, seeing as you have to do it to carry on with the game, here's the Resident Evil Piano puzzle solution.

Resident Evil Village piano puzzle solution - the notes to play

If you walk up and down the keys you'll see a red note moving up and down the music, level with the first note. When it hits the right one it'll lock in place, and a red dot will appear level with the next note, and so on. It's not too hard, after a couple of pokes at the keyboard, to narrow down the distance between the note you're playing and the one you need. However, up there we've numbered the keys you need to press, in the order you need to press them. Follow those numbers and you'll play the correct melody and complete the puzzle.

What isn't initially clear when you start is that you can't really 'fail' this puzzle. In theory you can just move up and down the keys until you've made all the notes red, with no fear of resetting the puzzle and having to start over. It's not the fastest way through it but it'll get you there in the end.

Getting the Iron Insignia Key

When you've played all the notes the puzzle will stop, some music will play, and a door will pop open in the front of the piano. Inside you'll find the Iron Insignia Key. Not only is this a useful key you'll need to progress through Castle Dimitrescu, but it'll open a few important doors back in the village. So it's worth a little musical torture to get it.

How to solve the Resident Evil Village bell puzzle and ring all five bells

The Resident Evil Village bells are part of a puzzle in the Atelier in Castle Dimitrescu. This room has five bells you need to find and shoot to make chime, before you can continue with the game. While three are pretty obvious, there's a couple that can be tricky to find if you don't spot them straight away.

Making all five Resident Evil Village bells chime is an essential part of the game, and you won't be able to leave the Atelier in Castle Dimitrescu and move on with the story until you do. Solving the Resident Evil Village five bells puzzle is relatively straightforward in theory – find and shoot five Resident Evil bells to ring them all. However, as we mentioned a couple are well hidden and if you don't seem them straight away you'll likely miss them for ages. So if you are struggling with this puzzle, we we can show you where to find all the Resident Evil Village bells and how to make them chime.

How to solve the Resident Evil Village Bell puzzle in the Atelier

See the small note on the painting in the middle of the Atelier? It says: "Let the five bells of this chamber ring out", and it's the only hint you'll get. It's also a bit misleading though, as you must only make the five bells ring. There's no need to let them 'ring out' (which, in fact, they won't). After finding and hitting one, a small flame will start burning just above the bell. Here's where to find them all:

Resident Evil Village Bell 1

You may have already spotted this one, as it's fairly easy to find. Just look to your left while standing in front of the painting in the middle of the room, and you can see it besides the white bust. There's no need to use a bullet; you can easily reach it with the knife.

Resident Evil Village Bell 2

Look at the opening in the wall behind the painting in the Atelier. Between the cogs, you'll see a large swinging bell. The only way to hit it is with a bullet, so it's time to draw your handgun. Make sure you get the timing right; if standing close by, there'll be less chance of wasting a bullet.

Resident Evil Village Bell 3

Now, turn your back to the cogs and the swinging bell. On the other side of the Atelier, you'll see a cabinet with a tiny bell on top. You'll need another handgun bullet to make it swing.

Resident Evil Village Bell 4

If you look up, you'll notice a chandelier hanging from the ceiling. The fourth bell is on top of it, but you can't see it from here. Walk up the wooden stairs, and you can just see the top. If you miss it but hit the chandelier, it will start to swing and you can easily hit the bell again.

Resident Evil Village Bell 5

That leaves the fifth and final bell, which you can hit from the same position on top of the wooden staircase. You can see a window from here; the bell is outside. It's fairly big, and can easily be shot with your handgun.

What happens after the Resident Evil Village bell puzzle is solved?

When the five bells are all ringing, you can proceed to the next area of Castle Dimitrescu. The large portrait on the wall swings open, and you're free to go through. We won't tell you what awaits you next... but good luck up there!

8 Resident Evil Village Tips & Tricks That Will Help You Survive the Horror

Keep Moving

Resident Evil Village is a first-person shooter, but it's not that kind of first-person shooter. You'll fight monster hordes, but there's little cover to hide behind. Certain areas have moveable objects that can block doorways, so you should use them to slow the monster flow toward your position, instead of ducking behind them.

Keep moving and shooting. Most enemies have stop-and-start attack patterns, meaning you can get some distance and safely do damage from range. In addition, many encounters take place in combat arenas with ammo and traps strewn around the playfield, so keep your eyes open and don't stand still.

Choose Your Weapons Wisely

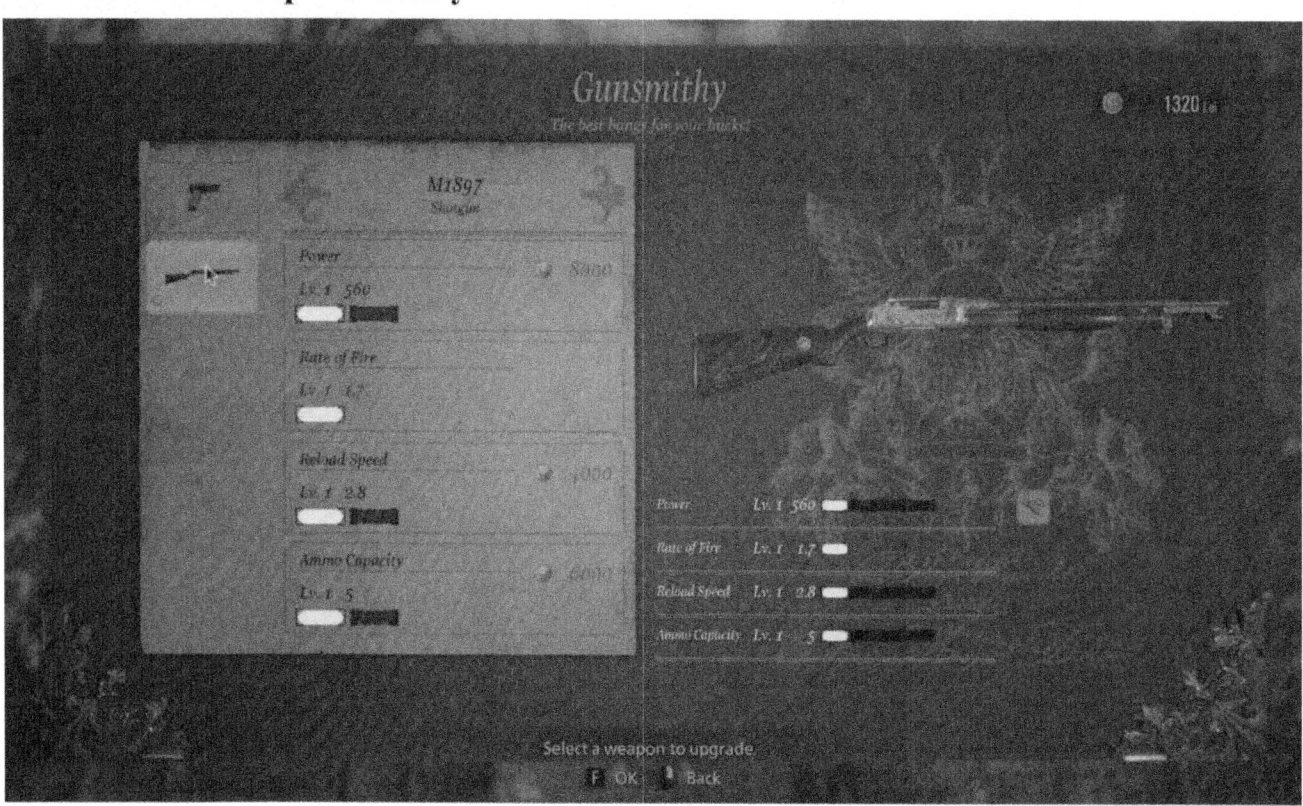

Storage space is at a premium in Resident Evil Village. While ammo and consumable items tend to take up one or two slots in your inventory, weapons can take up anywhere from six to twelve slots. There's no item stash in Village, so the only storage space available is what's in your personal inventory.

Beyond that, weapon upgrades cost Lei, the in-game currency. You'll get Lei by selling the crystals you find around town and the crystalline body parts you retrieve from monsters and bosses. Weapon upgrades are prohibitively expensive, so you will only have enough money to upgrade a few weapons on each playthrough. Pick two favorites that suit your playstyle and focus on their upgrades.

In addition, you shouldn't upgrade the starting pistol and shotgun. You'll get better versions of those weapon types later, and weapon upgrades do not transfer from weapon to weapon.

Buy Storage Space Upgrades and Recipes

The Duke is Resident Evil Village's version of the mysterious Merchant from Resident Evil 4. He'll pop up from region to region, offering his wares and a convenient save spot. Although the Duke sells ammo, healing items, and weapon upgrades, your first purchases should be crafting recipes and more storage space.

Crafting recipes lets you craft additional ammunition from scraps and other materials. As a result, you won't need to rely on finding specific ammo scattered around the village. You should also purchase at least the first storage upgrade. It's expensive, but it's well worth it.

Sell Treasure

Your best way to get more Lei for upgrades and other purchases? Sell treasure. You'll find crystals, trinkets, and crystalline body parts on dead monsters. Most of these can be sold with little issue. There's no reason to hold onto it.

Certain items will be listed at "Combinable" in their descriptions. In these cases, you must find the other items that can be combined with them. Once combined, you can sell the resulting treasures. For example, you can combine the head of a creepy doll with its body. You could individually sell either item, but you'll get more money for a complete doll.

Leave Your Food With the Duke

One way to get permanent upgrades in Resident Evil Village is to bring the Duke various types of meat to cook.

You'll get the meat from killing pigs, goats, fish, and chickens. The Duke has several recipes that give you permanent health and speed boosts, as well as recipes that reduce the damage you take from enemies.

The meat takes up space in your inventory, which is never good. That said, you can give the meat to the Duke, and he'll hold it.

You don't have to complete a recipe all at once; it'll still be there if you leave and return. So get rid of that meat, it'll only attract the undead.

Save Your Ammo and Explosives for Big Fights

As previously mentioned, ammo is at a premium in Resident Evil Village. You're thrust into heavy combat situations that require a great deal of gunfire. So don't waste your handgun bullets on breaking open boxes or hunting animals - use the knife.

Save the shotgun or your explosives for crowded situations, not one-on-one fights. And once you get the very powerful M1851 Wolfsbane Magnum, save those valuable bullets for boss fights. Ammo management is key in this game.

Consult Your Map

Resident Evil Village's map gives you a lot of information. Not only does it have icons for major treasures, it also lets you know when you've completely cleared a room. Rooms are colored red when you first discover them, but they turn blue once cleared.

To clear a room, you must find all the interactable items within the environment. Use this as a handy way to scour rooms for every bit of useful material.

Play It Again

You've beaten Resident Evil Village? Great! But you're not necessarily done with the game. On your first completion, you'll unlock the Extra Content Shop, which will be available under the title menu's Bonuses section.

As you play through Resident Evil Village, you'll get Content Points (CP) for completing objectives, such as beating the game on any difficulty level, collecting achievements, and upgrading weapons to their maximum capacities.

Once you have CP, you can unlock new perks in the Extra Content Shop. These perks include new weapons, infinite ammo on certain weapons, and the entire Mercenaries multiplayer mode.

You won't be able to unlock all the items via a single run, meaning you must play through the story campaign multiple times in order to unlock everything.

14 tips for surviving Resident Evil Village

Enemies react based on where you shoot them

Popping lycans in the dreamer is the goal, but they're not going to line up and wait their turn for a shell to the skull.

You'll need to manage whole crowds of these furballs, and letting your aim fall to a kneecap or hand can soften up the horde.

Shoot a lycan's hand and it'll drop its weapon, decreasing its attack range and lethality. Shoot 'em in the knee and they'll drop to the ground, which is effectively a lycan pause button that lets you focus on the nearest head. Some will shoot flaming arrows at you, and yes, you can shoot those out of the sky. Even cooler? Knock it down with a knife. Show them who the real leader of the pack is.

For a more classic RE survival experience, play on Hardcore from the start

Standard is tense but breezy. I only died twice and never felt like my resources were stretched too thin.

Hardcore is probably the sweet spot for those familiar with survival horror games who don't mind running out of ammo and dying more often. If you get excited thinking about resorting to the knife, Hardcore is the mode for you.

PSA: I'd avoid playing on the hardest difficulty, Village of Shadows, the first time around. Not because I don't believe in you, but because it places more challenging enemies saved for dramatic reveals in the late game into earlier encounters.

Mouse and keyboard users, here's a grenade launcher PSA

This might've been fixed for release, but it took me a long time to figure out. In order to change ammo types while using the grenade launcher, you need to aim (hold right mouse button) and then press the F key.

As of writing, it just says press F to change ammo. A bold-faced lie! But that's horror, you know? Can't trust your eyes.

Look ahead

In some areas you can spot enemies waiting in ambush, Dark Souls style. Get the jump on them, and by jump I mean shoot them in the head from very far away with your scoped rifle. Maybe lay out a mine or two if you're feeling saucy.

And look up

If you see a sparkle embedded in the wall, that's money. Shoot it and treasure will drop. You'll also see yellow birdcages in some parts of the world. Shoot them down for some money or ammo. It's almost always worth the ammo cost since that money's probably going towards better weapons or upgrades anyway. Why are shotgun shells hanging around in rusty old birdcages in some old evil castle, you ask? Shut up, nerd!

If the tight FOV is killing you…

Yeah, so there's no FOV slider in Village, which won't slide if you've got a certain monitor size and distance and limited capacity for motion sickness. I felt fine throughout, but if you need to broaden your perspective, read a damn book! Or just try out this RE8 FOV slider mod.

Sell your old weapons for newer, better ones

In my experience, every new set of guns was simply more powerful than the last. Village feels tuned towards pushing you into new weaponry on the first playthrough anyway, locking most weapon upgrades away behind piles and piles of cash. The new stuff will always do you well, and besides…

Don't craft items until you need them

I get it. You're topped off on shotgun ammo, but you've got the supplies to make some more. Why not make your bed, craft some more shotgun ammo just in case, you wonder? While you will need more eventually, it might not be what you need next. There's always some new scenario and strange monster lurking around the corner in Village and limited supplies to put 'em down with. Save your crafting supplies for making stuff on the fly. Chances are a landmine or pipe bomb or rifle ammo might serve you better in the next fight.

You can buy back your weapons, attachments and upgrades included

If you really miss your first shotgun (and who doesn't?!) you can buy it back, with all the previous upgrades and attachments. This is especially important in New Game Plus (see more on that below), since upgrading weapons completely unlocks the unlimited ammo option for purchase in the bonus store.

Prioritize inventory size upgrades

It can hurt to drop megabucks on a big bag, but you're going to have a lot of guns by the end of Village. And pipe bombs. And mines. And bags of raw animal meat. Don't risk leaving any valuable resources behind just because there's no room left between the trout filet and magnum.

Revisit old areas and make sure to explore thoroughly

Scan every location for stuff you might've missed. There are extra puzzles, hidden treasures, and secrets to uncover. And some of the secrets will try to kill you, so keep that shotgun primed. We're eating secrets tonight.

Stop! Combine before you sell

I get it. You're chasing that paper and you've got a huge haul of doll bodies to dump on the merchant. You might want to keep those doll bodies until you find the doll heads to match 'em though. The sell price on those suckers will soar. Before selling anything in Village, make sure it's not missing any pieces, denoted by a Combine option when you select it in the menu. If there's nothing to combine it with, well, get back out there and don't come back until you've got the doll heads to match. No one said life in the village would be easy.

Break windows, shoot crows, open outhouse doors! Follow your heart, child of chaos!

If you can break it or interact with it, chances are there's some kind of achievement attached. Break all the windows you can in the castle, shoot down five crows, open every outhouse door in the village - and plenty more, be sure to experiment! Dink around enough and you'll get a nice little bonus store currency payout once you've finished the game.

How to start New Game Plus

And you should, because it rules. You get to carry over all your weapons, weapon upgrades, items, treasure, and Ethan upgrades over to a brand new game, and on any difficulty you've unlocked. But like a man hiding in a closet from a horrific monstrosity sliming its way up and down the halls, New Game Plus does not leap out and make itself known.

To access the feature, you'll need to choose Load Game from the main menu, then scroll down to wherever your completed save game file is. Click it and you'll get the prompt to start a new game. Now breeze through Hardcore mode with all your powered-up gear and whatever wild, broken infinite ammo hand canons you unlocked in the bonus menu. Hardcore indeed.

15 Tips and Tricks to Keep in Mind

Blue is good

Regularly checking your map is a core part of most Resident Evil games, and so it is in Village too. This is a tip that those familiar with the series will know all too well, but if you're a newcomer, always keep this in your mind- if a room on the map is highlighted in blue, that means it's cleared, and you've done everything here you can do. If a room is red, there's still something there you haven't found, whether that's crafting components, ammo or items, or treasures.

Keen an eye out for the shiny stuff

Speaking of treasures- Resident Evil Village brings back the shiny, sparkling treasures of Resident Evil 4, and just like in that game, many of these are often hiding in plain sight. They could be stuck to the walls, to the ceilings, to rafters in nooks that can only be seen from specific angles. Always survey your surroundings carefully, and if you see something sparkling, make sure you shoot it down. The cash you get for collecting treasures is invaluable.

Some treasures can be combined

Again, just like in Resident Evil 4, some treasures can be combined with each other to make them more valuable. Don't immediately sell off every treasure you find- head to your list of treasures in the menu, and the game will tell you if a certain treasure can be combined with others. Fully completed treasure sets earn you significantly larger quantities of cash when sold to the Duke, so always keep that in mind.

Explore thoroughly

This should go without saying, especially in a Resident Evil game, but we're gonna say it anyway, because it's important to remember. From missable treasures to animals to new weapons to notes and logs to even some secret bosses, Resident Evil Village has a lot of stuff hiding behind optional content that you can miss entirely, so make sure that you don't rush through the game. Any time you enter a new area, explore it as thoroughly as possible.

There's more to explore each time you return to the village

In fact, you should explore thoroughly not only when you're entering a new area, but also when returning to older ones. You'll be returning to the village, which serves as a central hub, multiple times throughout the game, and each time, you'll be able to head to new sections that were previously inaccessible. From being able to unlock doors to being able to head to far off locations that you couldn't get to before, the village will expand each time you return to it. Every time you come back, make sure you take some time to explore it some more before you resume the main quest again.

Hunt all the animals

Animal hunting is a completely new mechanic in Resident Evil Village, and it's quite crucial. The Duke can cook up special meals to permanently increase your max health, guard defence, and movement speed- which, as you would expect, is very important. Animals are often hidden in secret and optional areas though, both in the village and in the locations that serve as the game's main "dungeons" (so to speak), so always keep an eye out for them. Checking your map often is a good idea- but remember that if your map is too zoomed out, spots where animals can be found won't show up on it. Oh, and one more thing- don't waste bullets on hunting animals. Use your knife.

Don't waste money on upgrading the starting pistol

Like Resident Evil 4, Resident Evil Village has you spending money to upgrade your weapons throughout the entire game. We'd recommend not immediately getting started on that though. More specifically, don't waste money on upgrading the pistol that you start the game with- you get a better pistol not long afterward, and it's better to save up and use your money to upgrade that instead.

Crafting shotgun or sniper rifle ammo is better than crafting pistol ammo

You'll be picking up crafting resources and using them to craft ammo throughout Resident Evil Village, but if you have a choice, it's better to use those to craft ammo for your shotgun or your sniper rifle than for your handgun. Handgun ammo drops are plentiful in the game, while the Duke also sells handgun bullets for pretty cheap prices. Sure, sometimes you might find yourself with little to no ammo, in which case you'll have no choice but to use your resources to craft handgun bullets. But if you can help it, prioritize other, more powerful ammo types.

Shoot crows

Just like Resident Evil 4, you can shoot down crows that you spot in your surroundings, and just like Resident Evil 4, they often drop cash. If you're ever short on money, shooting crows is a pretty good way to build up a decent reserve.

They don't drop massive quantities of cash, of course, and you also need to keep an eye on how much ammo you have and whether you can afford to waste it on shooting crows, but if you have dire need of money, they're a good last resort, if nothing else.

Shoot down the cages

Shooting crows might not always be worth it, but shooting cages almost always is. Often, you'll find small yellow bird cages hanging from trees or ceilings in Resident Evil Village. Every time you do, make sure you shoot them down. They always give you either ammo or crafting resources, which is always useful.

Priorotize inventory expansion purchases

Resident Evil Village brings back the Tetris-style attache briefcase inventory management of Resident Evil 4, and you can, of course, expand your inventory by purchasing briefcase expansions from the Duke. In fact, we'd recommend buying those as soon as and every time they become available. Expanding your inventory to make sure you can fit the weapons you acquire throughout the game (in addition to all the different ammo types and health items) is quite important, so prioritize these purchases over everything else.

Guarding is crucial

Guarding is not a new mechanic – Resident Evil 7 had it as well – but it's much more important this time.

You'll often be attacked by large mobs of enemies, which means you'll often find yourself cornered and surrounded. In these situations, guarding against attacks is crucial to avoid taking too much damage, especially if you increase your guard defence using the Duke's special meals. Properly timed guards also allow you to follow up by pushing enemies away, which can also give you invaluable windows to shoot staggered enemies while creating some breathing room for yourself.

Turn off aim acceleration

Bafflingly, Resident Evil Village has aim acceleration on by default. In case you don't know what that is, as its name suggests, aim accelerate progressively increases the movement speed of your reticle while you're aiming down sights.

It's an absolute nuisance, and makes aiming extremely difficult and messy, which can make most combat encounters unnecessarily tough and sloppy. As soon as you begin the game, head into the settings and turn off aim acceleration.

Turn off adaptive triggers

If you're playing Resident Evil Village on a PS5, you're gonna want to turn off adaptive triggers as well. The game doesn't use the DualSense's adaptive triggers as well as you'd hope- every so often, the trigger will jam, leading to either missing your target completely, or not being able to fire off a shot at all. It's just annoying. It gets in the way of enjoying the combat. Give it a try for yourself if you feel like it to see if you like the implementation better than we did, but we'd recommend turning it off in the settings as soon as you start playing.

Mercenaries tips

Resident Evil Village brings back Mercenaries after many years of demands from fans, and there are a few basic pointers you should keep in mind while playing it. For starters, cash is limited, so it's better to have two weapons in your inventory and focus on spending money on their upgrades rather than buying every weapon you possibly can.

The good thing about this is that that'll let you sell off ammo for guns you're not using. For instance, if you're going with a handgun-shotgun combo, you're free to sell off any sniper rifle ammo you find, which goes for a surprising amount of money- giving you more to spend on weapon upgrades for the guns you have in your arsenal.

10 Things Only Pro Players Know You Can Do In Resident Evil Village

Stun Lady Dimitrescu

Following in the footsteps of Jack Baker, Mr. X, and Nemesis, Lady Dimitrescu is Resident Evil Village's pursuit character. After collecting Dimitrescu's Key in the Castle, the lady herself will start chasing after Ethan. She's on the slow side and never runs, but her claws do a considerable amount of damage and her wide frame will block your path in tight space. While this won't help you in hallways, it's possible to stun Lady Dimitescu by shooting at her head. She'll stop to adjust your hat, giving you just enough time to lose her.

Quick Turn

Quick Turn is a skill that's been a part of Resident Evil since the third installment on the PlayStation, but it's also one newcomers tend to neglect on first playthroughs. By holding back on the analog stick and pressing Circle, Ethan will immediately turn around. Quick Turning is especially useful when it comes to dodging damage or simple repositioning. Quick Turning is always faster than strafing in a circle and something any RE vet will swear by.

Blow Up Samcas With Mines

Samcas are the flying, hooded infected who start popping up after getting to Castle Dimitrescu's rooftop. Samcas are introduced at the same time as the Sniper Rifle – one of the strongest weapons in the game – so most players will be inclined to kill them from afar. Not only is it possible to actually kill a Samca with a Mine, there's a Challenge for it in the Bonus Shop.

This is easiest done at the top of Castle Dimitrescu. First, place a Mine down in between you and a Samca. Pull out your weakest gun and aggro the Samca. As they fly towards you, pepper them enough times so they stagger and fall on top of the Mine. The Samca's body will trigger an explosion, usually killing them on the spot.

Guard-Push Combo

Building off the newly introduced Guarding mechanic from Resident Evil 7, Resident Evil Village adds Pushing into the mix. Pushing is a valuable skill players can use to create immediate openings in combat. Ethan can Push enemies by pressing L1 right after blocking an attack with Guard.

If timed correctly, Ethan will knock enemies away, causing them to briefly stagger. Not every attack can be Guard-Pushed, but it's a valuable Combo to learn.

Knock Out Weapons

Unlike Molded, the Lycan in Resident Evil Village often carry weapons with them. Usually they're just farm tools, but there are Lycan who wield swords and are even armored.

It's important to aim carefully since Ethan can actually knock the weapon out of an enemy's hand. Lycan are frantic enough where this is easier said than done, but managing to shoot a Lycan's weapon gives you the perfect opportunity to follow up with some free hits.

Safely Upgrade & Sell Weapons

Even though the weapon upgrade system is back, Village's interpretation isn't as elegant as Resident Evil 4. In RE4, every weapon had its own special skill that ensured even early game guns were viable on higher difficulties.

This isn't the case with Resident Evil 8, where new guns are almost always stronger than early-game weapons.

That said, smart players can use this to their advantage. Since guns rise in value as they're upgraded, you can use the profits from your old weapons to upgrade to the next model.

Revisit Castle Dimitrescu

Castle Dimitrescu is the standout area in Resident Evil Village, but it's only explorable for a very short portion of the story.

While you won't be getting back into the main keep, Castle Dimitrescu's depths can actually be revisited once you unlock the Crank.

Take the Crank to the Drawbridge near the altar and ride the boat back to the Castle outskirts where there will be an explorable crypt with plenty of goodies.

Blast Through House Beneviento

House Beneviento has quickly earned a reputation as one of the scariest areas in Resident Evil Village, but it's actually a fairly simple area to get through once the initial shock wears off.

House Beneviento is a very small area and only has a few items Ethan needs to pick up. Players can beeline straight to the basement to start the Mia puzzle in no time at all.

While the baby chase is still tense, you only need to hide from the baby twice and the chase itself is slightly scripted.

The boss battle against Angie isn't too challenging either. She'll always be found in her bedroom on the second floor the first time around, and then exclusively stick to the first floor for the next two rounds.

Farm Challenges

Beating Resident Evil 8 once unlocks the Bonus Shop and Challenges. Challenges are in-game tasks that award CP which can be used to buy weapons, Infinite Ammo, and other goodies in the Bonus Shop. Most Challenges are specific to certain set pieces, but several are dedicated to defeating enemies with different guns. By saving right before Heisenberg's Stronghold, you can keep clearing out the dozens upon dozens of Lycan before reloading. This makes it very easy to farm CP fast.

Kill Urias Early

Urias is a hammer wielding giant Lycan who's fought at the very end of the Stronghold by Ethan and again by Chris near the end of the game. Urias is one of Resident Evil Village's hardest bosses and he actually appears during the swarm at the start of the story. Not just that, Urias can actually be defeated here.

Keep in mind that you'll likely need to do this on New Game Plus and have prepared beforehand. Infinite Ammo from the Bonus Shop goes a long way and you'll want to exclusively fight back with your strongest guns: the Grenade Launcher, Sniper Rifle, and Magnum. Killing Urias early will be tough with so many Lycan around, but it's possible.

10 Things That Make No Sense In Resident Evil Village

Crazy Day/Night Cycle

When Ethan wakes up from the car crash, it's pitch black outside. This is great because it makes the scene extra spooky. He eventually finds a house and maybe spends ten minutes in there at max, depending on the player, before exiting to find it to be morning. How could the day/night cycle be that crazy in this part of the world?

Disintegrating Weapons

One of the most senseless things in this game, and in Resident Evil 4 (from which this game takes a lot of inspiration), is not being able to pick up weapons.

In Resident Evil 4 they just drop. In this game, they disintegrate along with the body. A body going into an ashen state upon death is weird enough, although they are monsters so it's a bit more believable. Ashen weapons is another story.

Inventory Issues

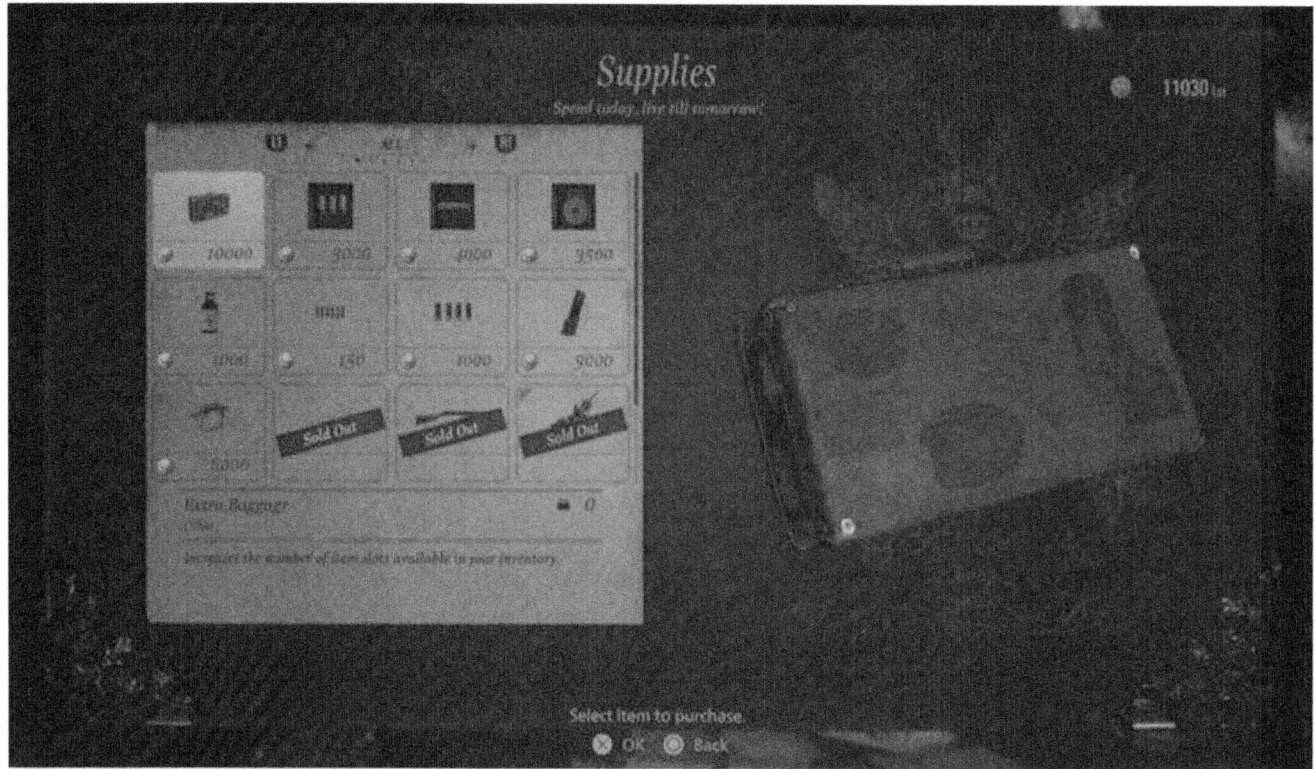

Video games with weight limits or limited inventory space is fine as long as it is consistent. In this game - and many games in the series - it is not. Ethan's usable space is determined by a suitcase that one presumably thinks he carries around. That's odd but, whatever - it's a video game thing.

Contrary to that, treasure and key items take up no space, which is good for the player but a head-scratcher all the same. This is especially true when considering bigger items Ethan carries around like the Giant's Chalice.

Might As Well Jump

So many problems in this game could be solved by a jump button. There are corners of the castle where Ethan can get trapped by one of the vampire witches.

He could escape by jumping down from the balcony overlooking the ground floor, but that's not an option. Simply climbing a fence from a locked gate is also impossible for Ethan it seems. This guy needs to work out more.

The Spiked Wheel Trap

There are plenty of traps in this game and in this series that no mere mortal should survive. One of the early examples is the spiked wheel that grinds toward Ethan after he escapes the Lycans Heisenberg sics on him.

The way to beat it is to hide in the corner and, at the right moment, Ethan will block the blades with his cuffs and break them. Vampire giants, fish monsters, and even magnetic powers make more sense than this solution.

Disarming Ethan

No one disarms Ethan whenever they capture him - Heisenberg doesn't in the beginning. Lady Dimitrescu doesn't in the castle. The only one that does is Donna, and it's questionable.

It appears as though she took his weapons and items away but it's supposedly just an illusion. The dollhouse portion doesn't make sense itself, but overall, the idea of the villains not taking away Ethan's stuff doesn't, either.

Vampire Weakness

Lady Dimitrescu and her three daughters seem invincible but all four of them have glaring weaknesses. The daughters are made up of bugs that, if frozen, will solidify their bodies, allowing them to be harmed.

Why move to this frigid region if that is a weakness? For Lady Dimitrescu, she is near impervious to damage except when Ethan strikes her with that dagger, triggering some sort of reaction to weaken her body. Why keep that on the premises?

Shot But Okay

At the beginning of the game, Ethan finds his first villager behind a curtain. This villager shoots off his gun, which seems to be straight ahead facing Ethan, and yet he takes no damage.

It could have been a blank or he could have swayed the shot at the last minute. It's not the most senseless thing in the game, but the way it plays out is certainly questionable.

Was Rose Really In Those Jars?

If one looks at Rose in the beginning of the game and then at the jars she's supposedly kept in, one could determine these jars are too small. That head alone shouldn't fit in these jars.

It's never really determined if her body really was split into four or not. It could have been a lie and maybe it was just the essence of these body parts that was extracted, like blood, or some other fluids.

Ethan Dies To Die Again?

This issue is more a problem with the script itself. Ethan dies by Miranda's hand - literally ripping out his heart, making the player think he's dead. If that were the case, it would have been super impactful.

The twist is that he has been a Mold creature this whole time, which raises so many questions. Without his heart, he apparently can't function for long, but he does have enough energy to rescue his daughter and sacrifices himself once more.

It's like having two encores. It wasn't needed.

10 Hidden Areas In Resident Evil Village Everyone Completely Missed

Luthier's House

Near the house with the red chimney which Ethan is tasked with finding after returning from Castle Dimitrescu, players may encounter the home of the musician Luthier, which is locked.

The key can be obtained after defeating Donna Beneviento, the second Lord of the village. It's in the Gardener's House, which players are all but forced to enter on the return trip from the manor on the cliff. Once found, return to Luthier's house and use the key. Pay special attention to a conspicuous child's drawing, which reveals the code to unlock a valuable treasure and an upgrade for the sniper rifle.

Riverbank Treasure House

After depositing all of the Rose flasks in the altar and acquiring the Giant's Chalice, Ethan will be able to return to the ritual site and access Heisenberg's factory. However, before crossing the bridge to get there, hang a right, use the crank to lower the bridge, hop in the boat, and head upstream to return to the base of Castle Dimitrescu's massive tower.

From here, enter a nearby torchlit alcove and solve the puzzle by lighting a Moroaica on fire and leading it into an unlit torch.

This will unlock the room at the end of the chamber, granting Ethan the valuable Golden Lady Statue.

Well Behind The Craftsman's Hut

In that same area at the base of Castle Dimitrescu, players may remember being unable to uncover the secrets of a well behind the Craftsman's Hut. Ethan now has access to the Well Wheel, which can be found in the village hut originally locked behind the Iron Insignia gate that you have to pass through to get to the hut with the red chimney. It can be used to bring up a ladder.

Inside the well, players will encounter a simple puzzle that, once solved, grants access to a small treasure trove that most won't want to miss out on.

Cannibal's Plunder

After crafting the six-wing unborn key, head up to the Lycan stronghold and bear left just before ascending that creepy-looking staircase. Here, Ethan will encounter a large barn constructed over a creek.

Inside, he'll come face to face with a giant wielding a large ax. He'll take quite a bit of punishment to put down and has the ability to summon Samcas, so he can be something of a handful. Using things like mines and flashbangs to stagger him can be helpful here.

After defeating him, knock the three locks off of the red door on the other side of the room from which Ethan entered and reap the rewards.

Mold Cave

Board the boat just below the bridge in front of the ceremony site that becomes accessible after getting the crank from Moreau and head downstream. This will take Ethan to a small landing where he can find the phantom fish, which is useful when crafting rare recipes.

Here, he'll also discover a cave overrun with black Mold. The cave was seemingly used by a member of Chris Redfield's team, and a laptop that's been left behind indicates that the Mold is nearly identical to that seen in Resident Evil 7. There are other worthwhile treasures here, as well as another nod to the previous RE game in the form of an antique coin.

Heisenberg's Quarters

After entering Heisenberg's factory, Ethan will be thrust into a massive network of steampunk-esque catacombs rife with terrors and treasure in equal measure. One of the most valuable treasures in the location can be found in Heisenberg's Quarters, which can be unlocked after crafting Heisenberg's Key in the Foundry.

When facing the forge, turn right and head up the stairs. From there, Ethan will encounter the locked door leading to Heisenberg's Quarters, which he had previously passed by. In it, he'll find a piece of Heisenberg's Hammer. The other part is hidden behind a bombable wall near the generator that was used to restore power to the area.

Factory Zipline

Just before using Heisenberg's Key on the door on the top level of the factory, turn around and find a break in the railing surrounding the platform. Here, drop down onto the large pipe below, and turn around and walk up to discover a small stash of treasure and ammunition.

From there, Ethan can use a zipline to travel to the other side of the room and eventually make his way back to the aforementioned door. It's not a huge discovery, but it can be a major boon for players struggling to defeat the intimidating Sturm boss.

The Beneviento Grave

Before encountering Donna Beneviento in the house by the cliff, Ethan must first trek an overtly creepy trail that culminates at the site of a large, conspicuous grave. At first, there's nothing that can be done with it, but, after defeating Donna, the player can return to the village and discover a small mausoleum near the Maiden of War statue has opened.

Inside, Ethan can find a broken piece of a grave. He can then take this back to the aforementioned Beneviento gravesite. However, this will spawn in another giant, as well as several other enemies, so it's best to be prepared before heading in.

The Foundry's Secret

Heisenberg's Factory is rife with secrets, though players will have to use their wits to find a few of them. In the foundry, just a few rooms past the generator, fans will encounter one of Heisenberg's drill-handed monstrosities springing from a shipping crate.

Rather than killing him, players must lead him down the nearby staircase and into the nearby room, prompting him to attack the metal sheet blocking access to the other end of the area. Once this is done, the monster can be dispatched, and the player is free to access some extremely valuable late-game loot.

Castle Dimitrescu Dungeon Secret

After discovering the Iron Insignia key in Castle Dimitrescu, return to the dungeon Ethan initially escapes to after first encountering one of Lady Dimitrescu's daughters. After dealing with some Moroaicas, the player will find an unopened door bearing the Iron Insignia. Behind it is the treasure the mysterious map from the attic was attempting to point toward.

Once inside, solve a torch-lighting puzzle by blowing a hole in the nearby wall and killing some more enemies. Once this is taken care of, a nearby coffin will open, revealing the Azure Eye. This item can be made much more valuable when combined with the Silver Ring.

10 Things We Wish We Knew Before Starting Resident Evil Village

Replaying it again is one option which is handy for PS5 players as Sony released the game for free on their system. Some people just don't have the time even if it is free to play an entire game over again. Thankfully this sequel has a recap. What else should players be aware before getting into the game and for the first couple hours?

Difficulty Options

Most Resident Evil games have difficulty options, but that's not always the case. For that matter many AAA games don't have them like another recent horror adjacent PS5 game, Returnal. Those with a weak stomach to the more hardcore survival aspects of this series can be rest assured there is an easy mode along with a standard and hard option. Pick carefully though because they can't be switched out.

Don't Explore The Village Until You Get The Knife

While it might be tempting to explore every nook and cranny in this game, as one should, there is a time and place for that. It'll be about twenty to thirty minutes before players get their first weapon, the knife.

After that point other stuff can be collected seemingly unlocking that ability. So exploring the village prior to the knife is a waste of time. Once Ethan enters the village, just follow the main path to the house with a fire outside. That's where the knife is

Run, No Seriously Run

The first werewolf zombie has to be taken down as it is basically a tutorial fight. The next few are optional and should be avoided in the village. All one needs to do is get onto a roof, and survive as long as possible. Then a cutscene will happen thus ending the raid. Not shooting as much as possible will save ammo so when the game says run, do it.

This Game Is Ammo Friendly

While it can be difficult to hold onto ammo, this game is pretty lenient. The easier the difficulty mode, the more ammo one will find as is usually the case in this series. Ammo can also be bought from the merchant, The Duke, for a tidy sum and it w can be crafted as well. One should also be aware that upgrading the ammo capacity on an empty gun will give players free ammo as well.

Upgrades To Focus On

On the subject of upgrades, here is what to focus on first. Emptying a gun and then upgrading the ammo slot is key. Overall though the first purchase one should save up for is the suitcase which expands the inventory. Cash is limited so don't go blowing wads of it if one can help it. One never knows when cash may be needed.

Don't Sell Your Food Ingredients

After the castle players will start to be able to kill animals like fish and chickens. Doing so will net them meat. While the game says to sell it to the merchant, that is misleading. The Duke will indeed buy it but it's not worth much. After an hour or so roaming around the village the second time, The Duke will eventually unlock his cooking shop. That's when the meat should be sold which will be used for ingredients to make dishes that will upgrade Ethan's stats like health.

Clearing Maps

A carryover from the recent remakes in the series like Resident Evil 2 is color coded maps. If the map is red then that means there is an item still there to grab. If it is blue one needs not to explore. What should one do if a room is completely picked over but still red? Look above. There might be something shiny to shoot.

Other Uses For Photo Mode

On its own, the knowledge of a photo mode might be helpful to know going in. However, that's not the cool part of it as the general use of it is not that robust. What is useful then is pausing the game in photo mode and then looking around a room for a solutions. This can be key to look into a boss' weakness or getting out of an incoming trap like the spike wheel early on.

Killing Flying Enemies

Toward the end of the castle, Ethan will find his way onto the roof. It's here that he will be bombarded with flying enemies. The sniper rifle is also unlocked here.

It might be tempting to snipe these enemies from afar but don't. Killing them near and by a surface means that they will drop an item to grab. Sniping them out of the sky negates that reward.

Use Headphones

This might be an obvious tip to give, but wear headphones. If one has a surround sound system that's great but more people probably have headphones. Just like Mr. X and Nemesis from the recent remakes in the series, there will be enemies constantly chasing Ethan. Putting on headphones will help players figure out their distance to them and or make them be aware of enemies near in general.

Printed in Great Britain
by Amazon